FREDERICK ELWELL
R.A.

1870 — 1958

by

Val Wise

HUTTON PRESS

1989

Published by the Hutton Press Ltd.
130 Canada Drive, Cherry Burton, Beverley
East Yorkshire HU17 7SB

Printed and bound by
Clifford Ward & Co. (Bridlington) Ltd.
55 West Street, Bridlington, East Yorkshire
YO15 3DZ

ISBN 0 907033 90 3

ACKNOWLEDGEMENTS

I would like to thank Sybille Cole, Margaret Garbett, Tom Collins, C. S. Deans, Raymond and Ted Elwell, Mrs. C.Hobson, Wendy Munday, William Oliver, Kenneth Pape, Peter Robinson, Jack Skinner, Lesley Tucker, Richard Wilson, the Antwerp Academy, the Royal Academy, Beverley Borough Council, Ferens Art Gallery, Lincoln School of Art, and many others who in various ways helped to make this book.

Val Wise,
Beverley,
September 1989.

LIST OF ILLUSTRATIONS

(List continues on page 6)

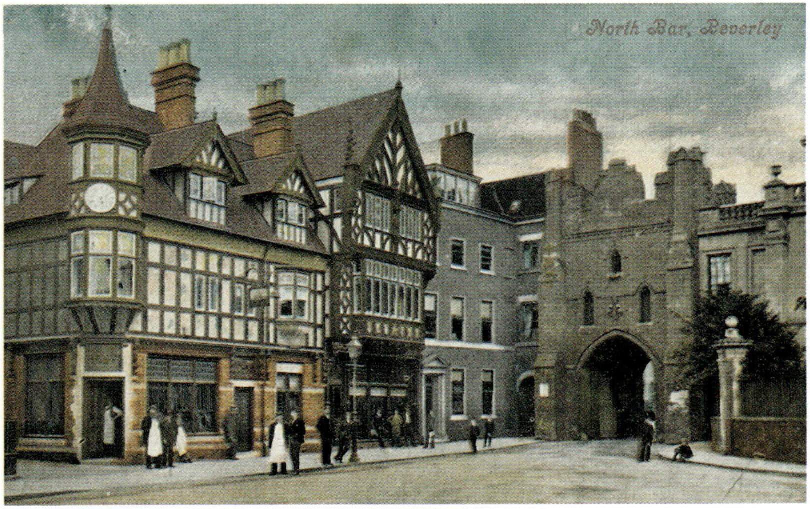

2. North Bar Beverley, with the Bar House and numbers 2, 4, 6 & 8 North Bar Without.

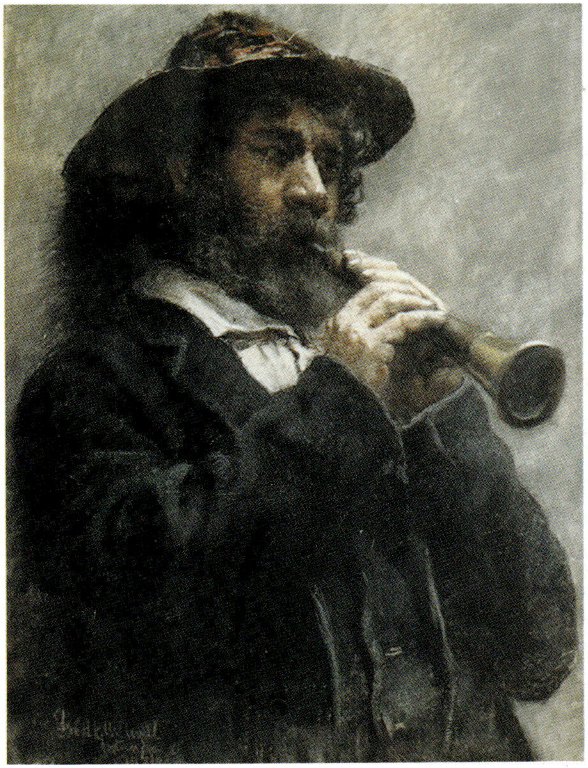

4. "The Trumpet Player" is a pastel, done when a student in Antwerp in 1890. Photograph courtesy of Alison Balding.

Fig. 18: *Castle of Les Baux* by Mary Dawson Elwell.

Fig. 19: *The Horse Tent*, courtesy of Beverley Art Gallery.

Fig. 20: *King George V* (1932), reproduced by gracious permission of Her Majesty the Queen.

Fig. 21: Photograph of Fred as the Earl of Hastings (1937), courtesy of Peter Robinson, Playhouse Cinema.

Fig. 22: *The R.A. Selection and Hanging Committee* (1939), courtesy of the Royal Academy.

Fig. 23: *A Wheelwright's Shop* (1945), courtesy of Beverley Art Gallery.

Fig. 24: *A Sheriff's Luncheon* (1946), courtesy of Hull City Council.

Fig. 25: Saturday Market (1935), (private collection).

Fig. 26: Photograph of the Trinity Lane Studio find (1976).

Back Cover: *The Curiosity Shop* (1930), courtesy of the Harris Museum & Art Gallery, Preston.

FREDERICK ELWELL, R.A. (1870-1958)

"Not only a painter but a man of culture, fond of books and of music and of all the good things of life. He was a master of the forgotten art of living". So ran the obituary to Fred Elwell by W. Oliver of *The Yorkshire Post* in 1958.

Fred was 87 when he died and his life spanned years of dramatic changes. His Victorian childhood was dominated by his father's enthusiasm for craftsmanship, civic duty and the theatre. From this Fred went on to experience the art revolution in Europe, to mingle with London society and to benefit from patronage by British aristocracy. Nevertheless, Fred's fundamental admiration for the artisan and sincere love of his home town, Beverley, always prevailed.

Although Fred was a prolific painter and well-respected, he is not widely known and there has been very little written about him. He had 190 paintings hung at the Royal Academy and many municipal galleries have examples of his work. The Ferens Art Gallery, Hull, has six paintings, and of course the Beverley Art Gallery has over fifty paintings by Fred and his wife, Mary.

Fred's generosity in giving oil sketches as gifts means that many families in the East Riding of Yorkshire count an "Elwell" among their heirlooms.

Frederick William Elwell was born in Beverley in the East Riding of Yorkshire on 29th June, 1870. He was one of six children and the youngest son (Fig.1). His father, James, was an outstanding personality in Beverley. He came to the town when his father was employed by Jackson and Bean in building the Hull and Bridlington railway. Having served his apprenticeship with May and Loftus, a firm of cabinet-makers in North Bar Within in the 1850's, James went to London and was employed in "some of the best establishments". He settled back in

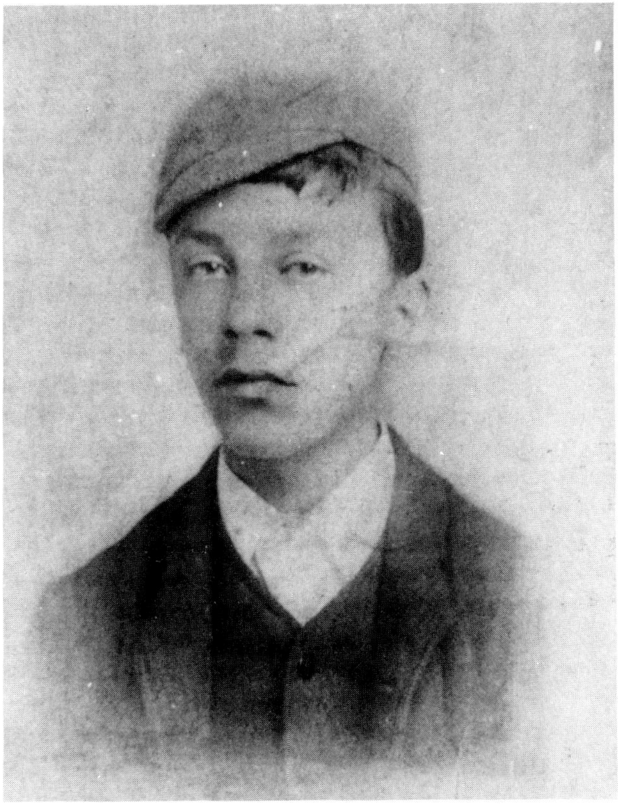

1. Photograph of Fred as a boy (privately owned).

Beverley as foreman to Mr. Richard Jameson to whose business he succeeded. A commission from Sir Gilbert Scott gave the firm a boost. This was to carve the choir screen in Beverley Minster to Scott's design and was based on the adjoining sixteenth century choir-stalls. The prestige derived from this work was very encouraging to James and his six assistants. He went on to employ sixty craftsmen and was responsible for much of the ornate wood-carving on the houses in North Bar Without as well as in Lincoln Cathedral, Holy Trinity Church, Hull and restoration work in Driffield Parish Church. The firm also built the carved case for the organ in Sydney Town Hall.

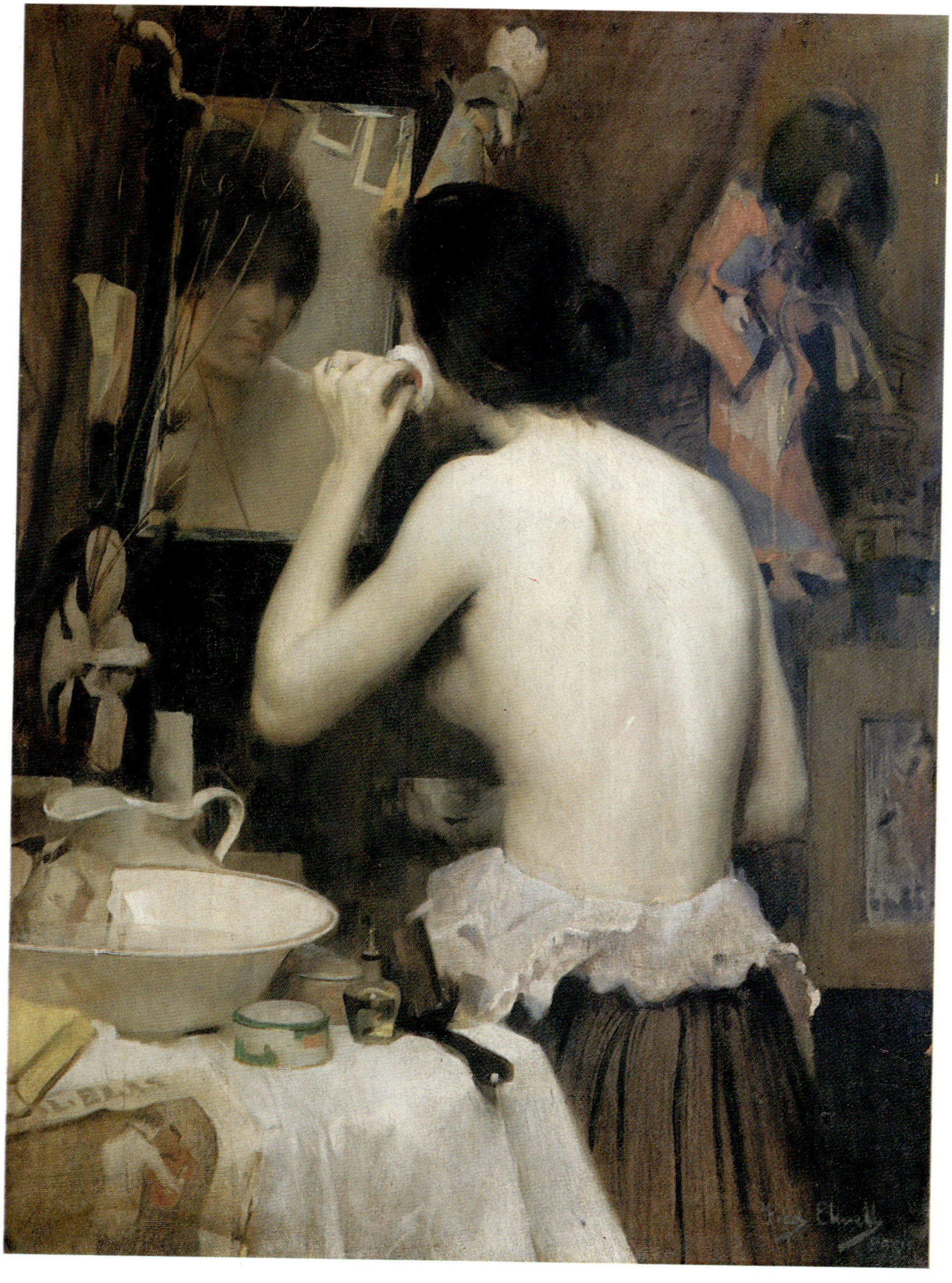

6. "Leonie's Toilet" was exhibited at the Royal Academy in 1895 as "Dolls" and re-exhibited in 1950. Reproduced courtesy of Beverley Art Gallery.

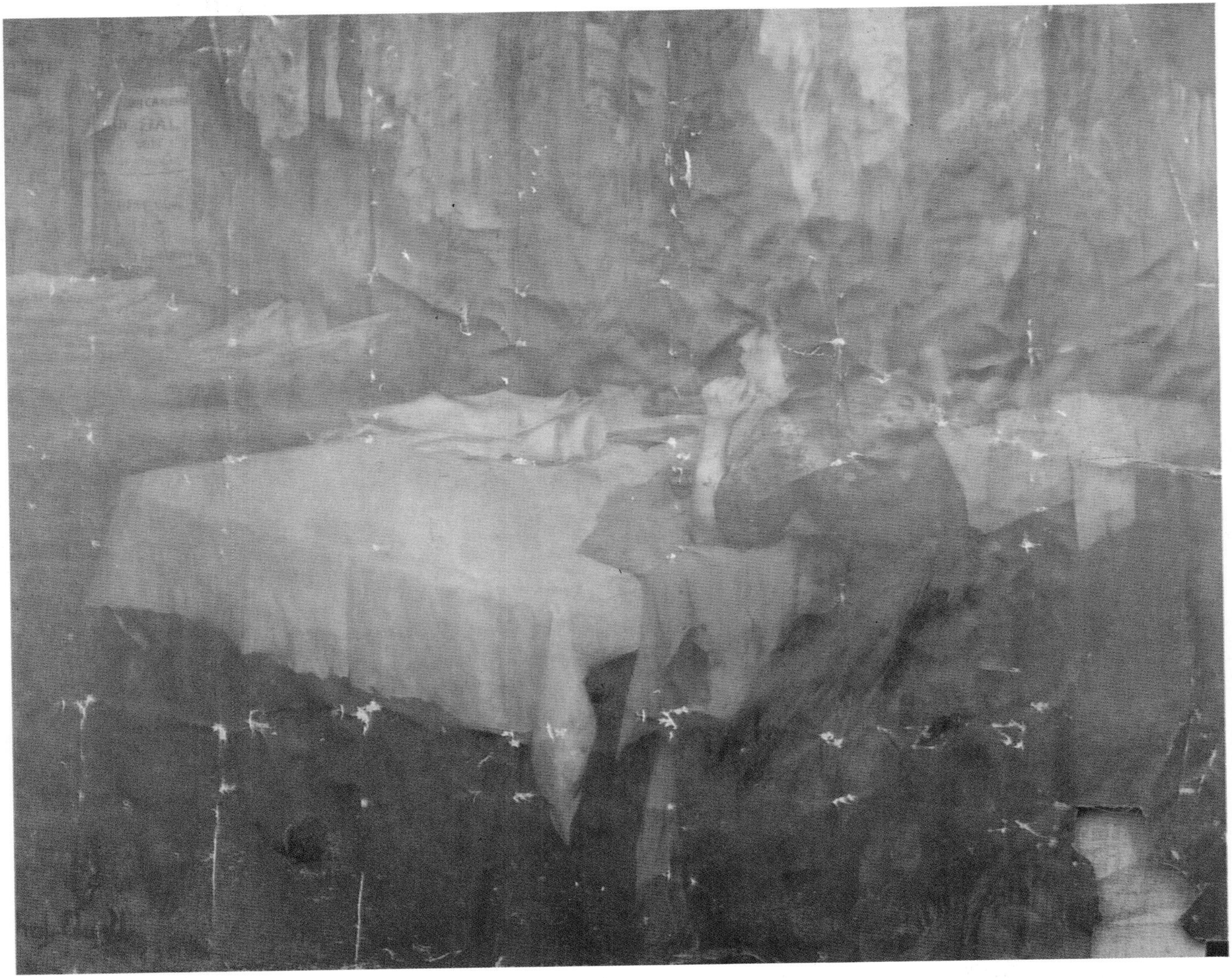

8. *"The Day After the Fête" was exhibited as "Le Lendemain de la Mi Carême" in Paris in 1895 and in Fred's Wood Lane exhibition in 1899 (private collection).*

The Elwell's former house, 4 North Bar Without, now a winebar, and the buildings next door, have frontages produced by the Elwell firm (Fig.2) in 1892. One carved door-head shows Disraeli ready to give up liberal principles in favour of popular opinion and is entitled the *Political Cheapjack*. James himself was a liberal turned Tory. His foreman, W.J. Thorley, has his name inscribed over the door of the woodcarver's shop in the background. Another carving is of a benevolent Gladstone restraining four leashed dogs — the Labour, Nationalist, Radical and Parnellite parties and is entitled *Will They Work?*

James was twice Mayor of Beverley and Fred faithfully recorded the event in 1900 and 1901. Highly respected in the community, James was one of the founders of the Beverley Building Society and a Freeman of the town. He served for seventeen years on the Library Committee and was involved in the inauguration of the Art Gallery above the Library, now housing many of his son's works. He was also an art collector and an enthusiastic theatre-goer, and was acquainted with Ellen Terry. Pinewood, a house in North Bar Without, has a doorhead depicting another theatrical acquaintance, J.C. Toole, a famous comedian of the time. He is portrayed as the toymaker in *Cricket on the Hearth* who will go as "near nature as he can for sixpence". James also painted a little and some of his water colours are still in existence. He belonged to the Beverley Photographic and Sketching Society.

Enormously proud of his son, James willingly posed for many pictures. How prepossessing is his patrician head in the *Last Purchase* (private collection) (Fig.3) when at the age of 85, he is portrayed examining a piece of porcelain at a table in the Bar House, his son's home for 42 years. It was this picture in 1921 that really made Fred's name and led to many commissions.

James died in 1926 at the age of 90 at Park Villa, York Road, after only a few days' illness, although he had been confined to a bath chair for his final few years and was a familiar sight being pushed around the town by a daughter or nurse.

Of his other children, John the eldest followed his father into the cabinet-making business. Bernard became Countess Dysart's agent in Scotland and sat on Peebleshire County Council. Edward was an estate agent and auctioneer in Beverley and Fred, of course, became a Senior Royal Academician. There were also two sisters, Frances and Maggie, who often modelled for Fred.

In a family where art appreciation was second nature, Fred's flair was soon discovered and he was sent at the age of 15 to Lincoln School of Art. He had lived for a time with his grandmother in London and was used to being away from home. James accepted that painting was a profession for which sound training was necessary and Lincoln seemed a sensible choice as Margaret Elwell, James' youngest sister, was then Principal of the Lincoln Training College for Women.

Art master, George Webster, the brother-in-law of Sir George Clausen R.A., trained his students in the *Beaux Arts* tradition. Fred was obviously a dutiful student because he was awarded monetary prizes totalling £17.2s. during the four years of his stay in Lincoln. He shared the prestigious Gibney Scholarship with four other students, receiving £5. A still life of fish won the Queen's Bronze Medal, open to all the schools in the country, but for which, he said "I might have been a house decorator!" The Lincolnshire Chronicle of 1889 praised the picture as being painted with *remarkable fidelity, the colouring of the boiled lobster the smoked herring, etc., being very rich and effective.* Other prizes won by Fred were for perspective, drawing from life and the antique, and it seems that whatever he learned at this time he learned well. He stayed at Lincoln from 1885 until 1889.

Later in 1889, Fred travelled to Antwerp to further his studies, encouraged by his family. He found lodgings in the Mutsaardstraat and attended life classes at the Royal Academy of Fine Arts, along with 2,000 other students. Antwerp's tradition of intricate interiors with strong echoes of Pre-Raphaelitism may have been where Fred found inspiration for his intensely realistic interiors such as *Inventory and Valuation for Probate* (Bournemouth Art Gallery), *Bric-à-Brac* (Usher Gallery, Lincoln) and *The*

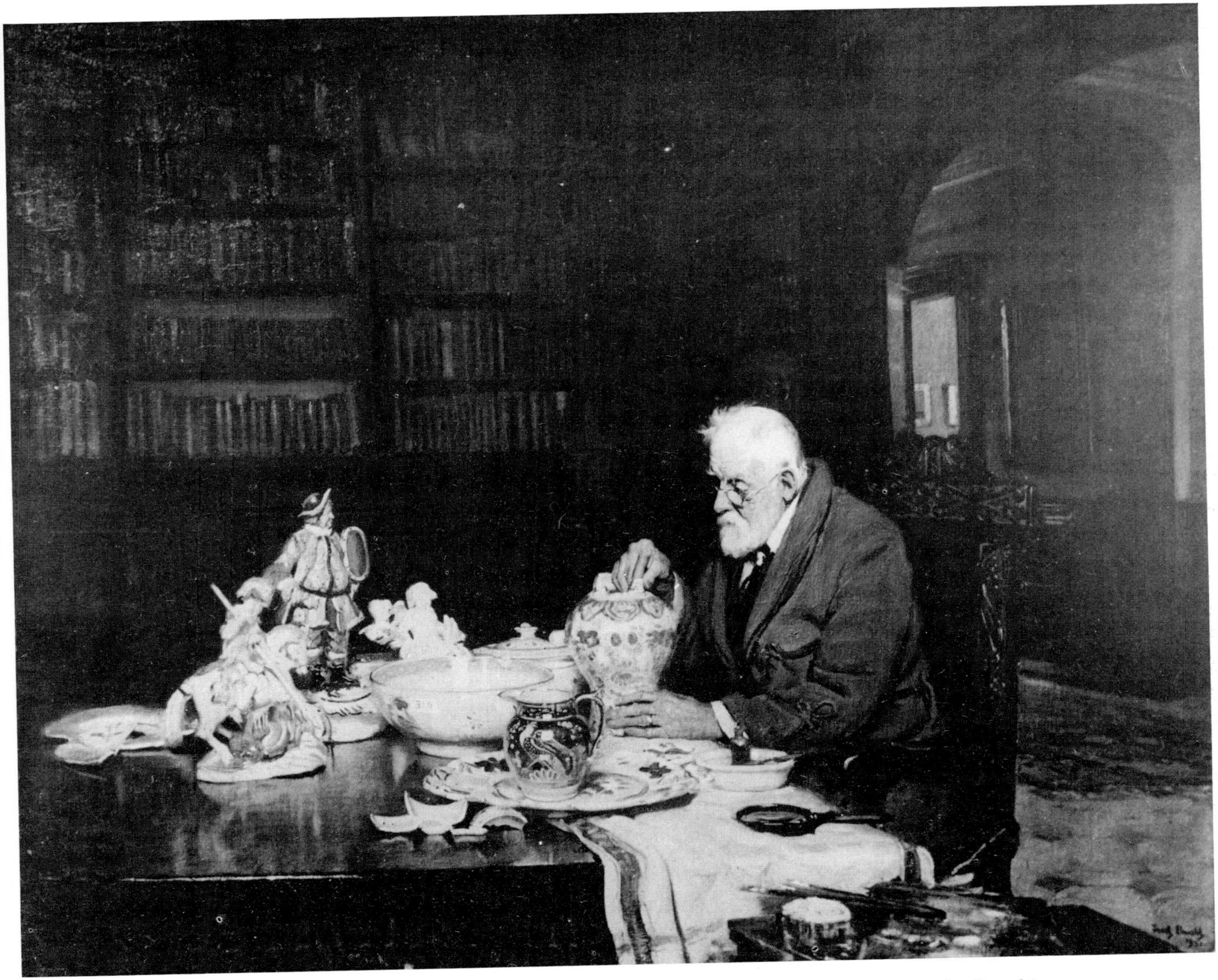

3. "The Last Purchase" was exhibited in 1921 at the Royal Academy and was Fred's first big success (private collection).

Curiosity Shop (Harris Museum and Art Gallery, Preston) (Back cover).

His interiors are not absolutely accurate records. For instance *Arden's Vaults* has extra pillars, the floor of *7 Hengate* has an added diamond pattern and the *Birthday Party* has a lot of artistic licence.

Fred would be commissioned to paint family groups set in a country house interior and then would extend his working sketches into other narrative paintings or conversation pieces, perhaps animating them with friends, relations or servants. Invariably an open door or obliquely placed window allows sunlight to splash into his interiors with an abrupt change of tone adding interest to an otherwise mundane scene. Elwell could achieve great depth by perspective lines made by ceilings and walls, as in the *The Long Gallery, Thorpe Hall* (private collection) and *Police Court* (Guildhall, Beverley). By looking through archways or doorways, there is a remarkable three-dimensional illusion as in *Another Country House and Contents for Sale* exhibited at the Royal Academy in 1948. Fred had been to the sale of Cave Castle at South Cave, near Beverley and created the painting from memory and a few sketches on scraps of paper. It sold for £210. The house was said to be in danger of being shipped completely to America. Luckily this did not happen and it is now a hotel.

There are several pastel portraits dating from his time in Antwerp (Fig.4) which owe a lot to Rembrandt's tones and use of light. Another Dutch influence can be seen in Elwell's still lifes. He shows great skill in depicting reflections and the fish, succulent hams and game are subjects upon which the Dutch mercantile classes traditionally loved to gaze!

After gaining a silver medal of honour for drawing at the Antwerp Academy, Fred left for England in 1891.

The England to which Fred returned was witnessing the growth of artists' colonies, notably at Newlyn in Cornwall and Staithes in North Yorkshire, both of which were visited by Fred and friends Laura and Harold Knight.

The sale of several portraits and landscapes during a stay in London helped to finance a period in Paris, the magnet for so many English artists at that time. Sir William Rothenstein, Charles Conder, Sir William Nicholson and Harold Knight were all in Paris around this time as well as Fred's great friends, Richard Jack and John Hassall. Hassall's portrait of Fred (Fig.5) in Paris shows a carefree young man and perhaps justifies his reputation as a *bit of a lad*. Fred's studio was just off the Boulevard Montparnasse in the Rue Campagne Première, where Picasso almost settled in 1900. Fred joked about having to learn to cook omelettes and living on beans but he was hardly the typical starving artist, having enough money to enable him to travel around France, painting and sketching, sometimes in the company of Richard Jack. He was glad to escape the hard winter of 1895 in the north of England when several soup kitchens opened in Beverley and hundreds of people queued with their containers. Tobogganing on the Westwood in up to 28° of frost was a very popular pastime with many Beverlonians, including Fred's family.

Meanwhile, Fred was finding Europe at its picturesque best with much land going out of cultivation every year. With the increased use of cars and trains, rural areas were more accessible to more people and meant a boom in landscape painting by professional and amateur artists.

Fred's scenes were pretty but unexceptional; landscape being a private experience seemed rather alien to Fred's sociable nature. Prices for his landscapes have varied tremendously. In 1972, *A Footbridge at Vaison de la Romaine* was sold for £180 whilst a similar one had been won in a raffle for a shilling!

Fred attended the Academy Julien, in the Rue du Faubourg, St. Denis, the second largest atelier in Paris after the Beaux Arts. Bernard Romaine Julien had had an adventurous career. He had been a prize fighter. To raise money in 1860, he hired a studio, calling it an *Académie de Peinture*. Unfortunately this did not attract customers until he persuaded a number of well-known painters and sculptors to act as visiting professors. Most of the Nabis, Gaugin's disciples, worked there as well as Matisse, Derain and Léger. Russians, Turks, Egyptians, Serbs and Americans came together to create a cosmopolitan

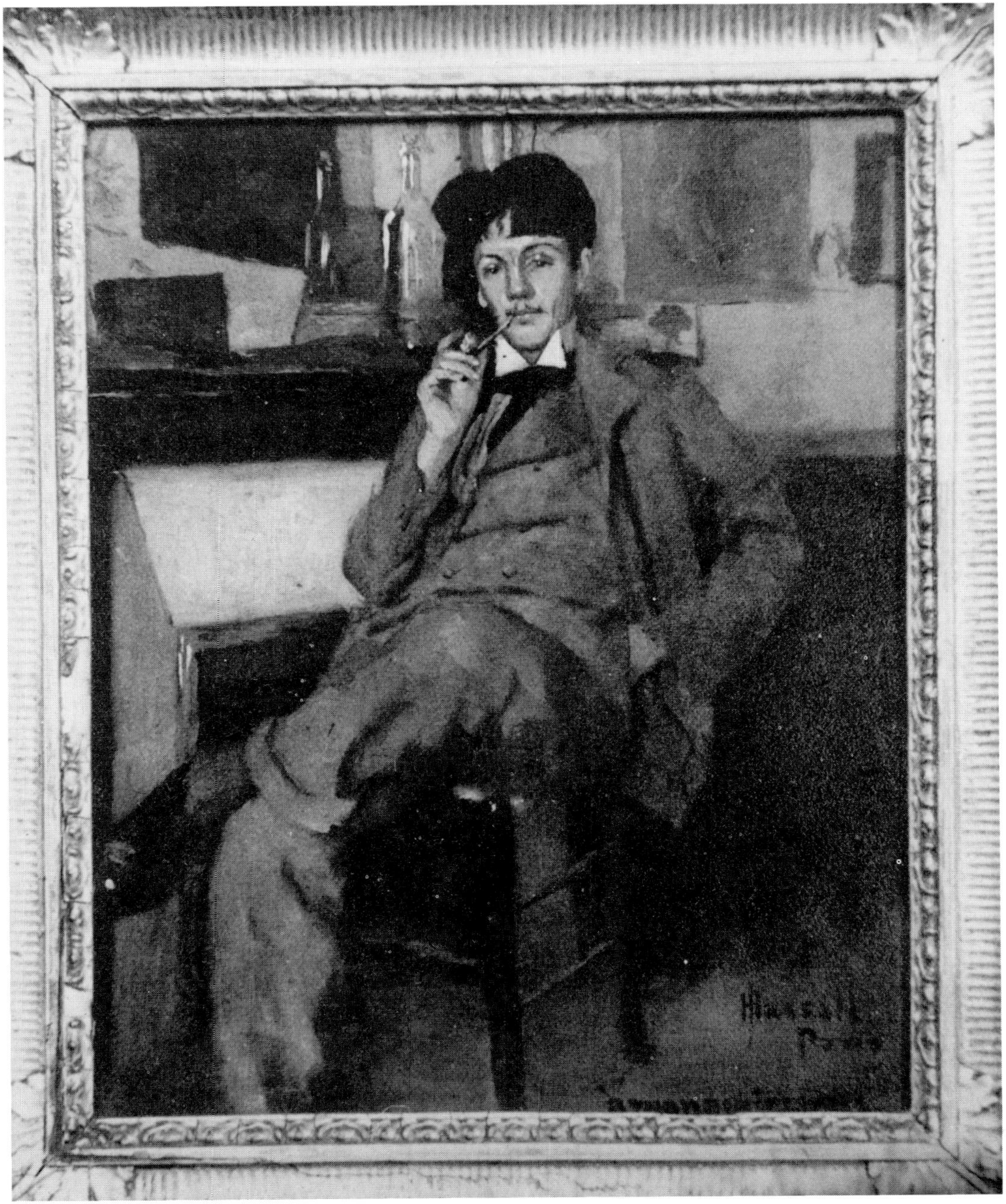

5. John Hassall's portrait of Fred as a student in Paris, inscribed "A mon ami F. Elwell" (private collection).

atmosphere. Notwithstanding the artistic revolution going on all around him, Fred's instincts led him to dismiss the Impressionists as a lot of drunks and drug addicts! He said that he could knock off two or three Picassos before lunch. Most masters at the Beaux Arts made sure that their own styles and names were perpetuated by their students but at Julien's the only tuition given was the principal's admonition, *Continuez toujours*, which Fred certainly did all through his life.

Dolls and *Disgraced* both painted in Paris, were exhibited at the Royal Academy in London in 1895. *Disgraced* is a melodramatic scene of a father banishing his dishonoured daughter from the family home. A *poetical* criticism of the picture appeared in the periodical *Pick Me Up* written by *Le Passant*:-

A very squalid kitchen scene
A sordid story of a woman,
Theatrical and rather mean
Conventional but very human.....

Several verses followed. *The Beverley Guardian* said that it was the best picture exhibited that year and speaks of the girl being *dishonoured but penitent.*

Dolls has had a chequered history: left with his landlord to pay the rent in Paris, it was found in a dirty condition in a junk shop in King's Road, Chelsea in 1949 by James Bateman R.A. and returned to Fred who re-exhibited it at the Royal Academy in 1950 under the title *Leonie's Toilet* (Fig.6). It is a study of a semi-nude backview of a woman making up in a mirror. Dolls are hanging on the tent wall beside her. The greenish shadows from the tent recur in some of the later circus pictures and many other paintings include some innovative greens. The magazine *Gil Blas* on the table beside the woman often contained art reviews. *The Beverley Guardian* of 24th August 1895 found it difficult to trace the connection between subject and title — "The proper title should be *The Toilet*". The painting, now restored, is in the Beverley Art Gallery.

The regular pay for models at the end of the 19th century was 7s. a day, including two meals, whether for face or figure. Female models who were not *fortunate* enough to marry the artist, usually ended by going on the stage, according to a contemporary writer.

Fred did not paint many nudes but another in the Beverley Art Gallery is the *Artist's Model* (1935) (Fig.7), a finely executed study with clear and creamy flesh tones.

Everything Fred submitted to the Paris Salon was accepted but for the next eight years his work was rejected by the Royal Academy. Despite several commissions and sales, Fred's main aim was to be accepted by the Establishment in the form of the Royal Academy and his early successes in no way made up for the discouragement he felt by his rejections. He stayed in London for a year or so along with thousands of other would-be painters, many of whom had, perforce, to become commercial artists. It was rumoured that Fred suffered a nervous breakdown at this time. He said he once found some of his old paintings in a junk shop and bought them for the frames, which were hard to come by.

He turned to more saleable themes unlikely to provoke comment. His scenes of a *slice of life* are such as could be seen by a disinterested passer-by glancing through a window. He made *nice* pictures. From commissioned portraits Fred made a living. The rich were prepared to pay for portraits. In 1903, a Raeburn fetched 14,000 guineas and a Romney, 9,400. Income tax was 1/- in the pound.

Back at Park Cottage in Beverley, he "set his teeth and made up his mind to succeed". The Old Quaker Chapel in Wood Lane was the venue for an exhibition in 1899. This got good reviews locally and a journalist praised the *wide variety of styles and subjects that his brush had produced.*

There were several landscapes and portraits in oil and pastel, some dating from his student days. *The Mace Bearer*, a pastel portrait of George Monkman aged about 90, was bought by Borough Treasurer, J. Hobson and it now hangs in the Guildhall. Disturbed by Mr. Monkman's pallor, Fred worried that he would die before the sittings were finished so kept plying him with brandy. His morose features were said to stem from his sad childhood as the

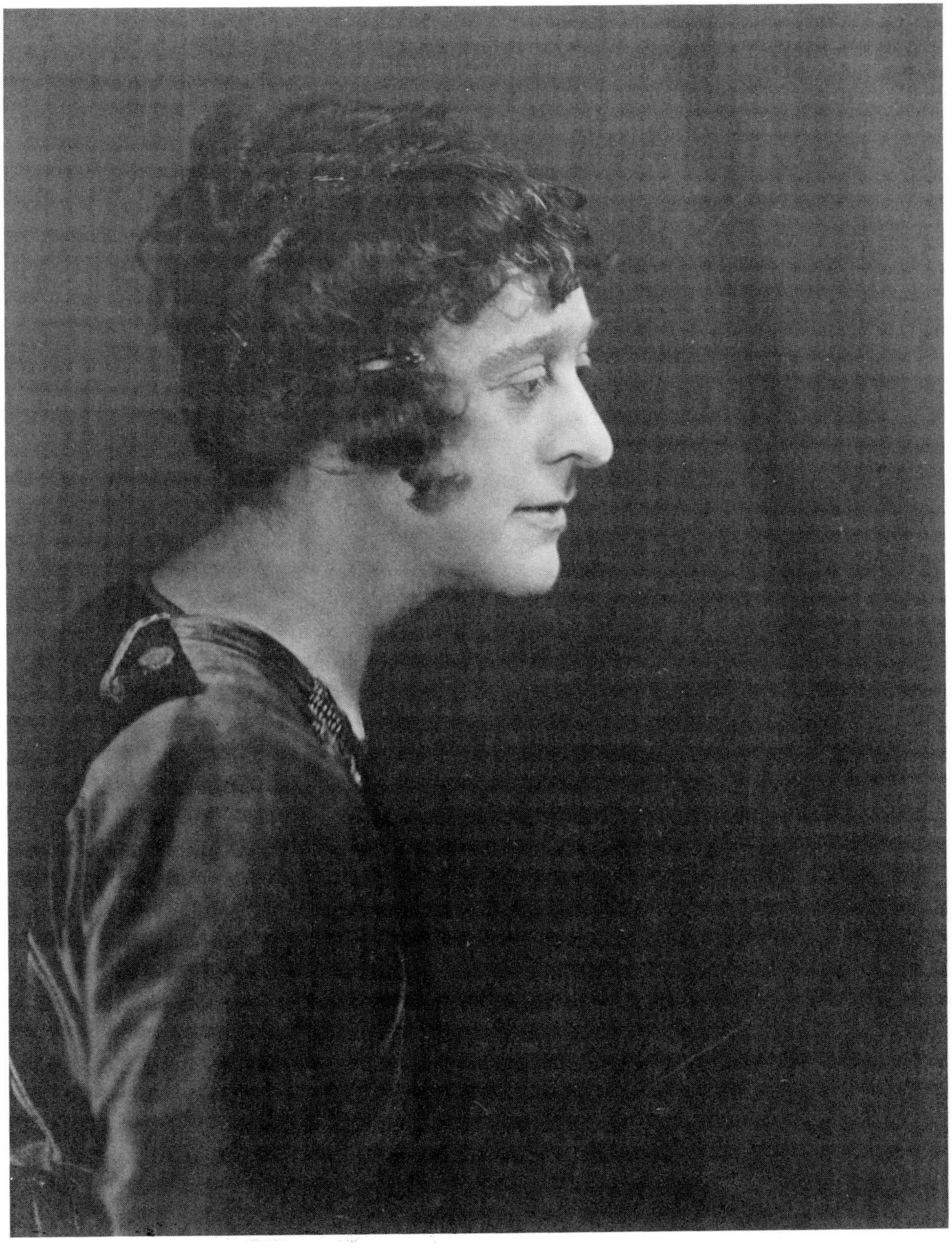

9. Studio photograph of Mary Dawson Elwell.

son of a Withernsea donkey man who lost all his donkeys in a fire. All his children had to be farmed out around the East Riding and thus George came to Beverley. His spirit is thought to linger still in the Guildhall.

Workhouse men were the models for *A Bit of Baccy* and *A Brown Study*. Fred's sense of fun comes through in his choice of titles, such as *All Things Come to the Man Who Waits* in which a waiter pours a glass of wine for himself and *Interval for Refreshment* with a musician resting on his 'cello and taking snuff.

A narrative picture which had been hung in the Paris Salon as *Le Lendemain de la mi Carême* and in Beverley as *The Day After the Fête* (Fig.8) was a *view from Parisian life representing one of the helpers of the Queen of Flowers at her work in the laundry*, clearly regretting the passing of the glamour of the previous day's fête.

The popularity of melodrama in pictures and songs was perhaps an outlet for the emotion stifled by the *stiff upper lip* mentality of the Victorian era; later, Hollywood took over dispensing sentiment for the masses.

Dr. William Stephenson, a surgeon and antiquarian of Railway Street, bought several landscapes and continued to encourage Fred in his early career, as did his brother Robert of Oak House, New Walk, manager of the Golden Ball Brewery.

After the success of the exhibition which attracted many townspeople, Fred settled back into the community. He became a Freemason in 1900, giving his profession as *Artist*, and was made Worshipful Master in 1908. He stayed with popular taste and eschewed the *-isms* in art, disliking, with his friend, Sir Alfred Munnings R.A., *the way art was going in this country*. He and Fred criticised the Ferens Art Gallery in Hull for the purchase of "... that bloody thing of Fitton's with the red table cloth... It shows what foolery is going on and what an influence K. Clark is having on those directors ....."

From 1911 Fred exhibited at the Royal Academy virtually every year until his death. A portrait he exhibited in 1904 was of Mrs. Mary Dawson Holmes, a pupil of his. Usually known as Mamie (Fig.9), she was the daughter of John Bishop, a shipping merchant, and was born and brought up in Lancashire. Fred helped look after Alfred Holmes, her first husband, until his death, and spent a lot of time at the Bar House, their marital home.

Fred and Mamie were married by special licence at Holy Trinity, Wandsworth Common on 28th September, 1914 by the Rev. J.G. Denison. They honeymooned in Scarborough which continued to be a favourite haunt of theirs. Some of their paintings of the town show the bomb damage suffered by the lighthouse during the First World War.

The Driffield Jam Factory (Fig.10) (private collection) and *Refugees in My Studio* (Beverley Art Gallery) were painted also during the war. Fred and Mamie stayed in a caravan near Driffield whilst doing some agricultural war work.

1914 was also notable for being the year when Fred was specially invited to contribute work to the Anglo-American Exhibition. The local papers reported that this indicated the high recognition which Fred's art had gained.

Fred was now extremely well-placed, with no financial worries, as his wife had inherited money from her first husband and from her tobacconist uncle, plus shares in Carreras and the Imperial Tobacco Company. However this did not stop her disliking the smell of tobacco. Fred smoked a lot, generally rolling his own (very badly, according to friends) and he would try desperately to conceal tab ends and to waft smoke away at her approach, or escape to the Trinity Lane studio for a surreptitious drag!

Trinity Lane was Fred's main studio. He installed a northern light on the top floor which was stacked with props, paint and canvasses, several paintings being underway at the same time. Fred kept regular hours at the studio working through until noon, breaking for a convivial lunch and returning to paint until the light went.

On several weekdays he met friends such as Dr. Davey, Alderman Schofield, Canon Tardrew, and Richard Whiteing at 12.15 p.m at the Beverley Arms for some stimulating conversation. The bar at the Beverley Arms

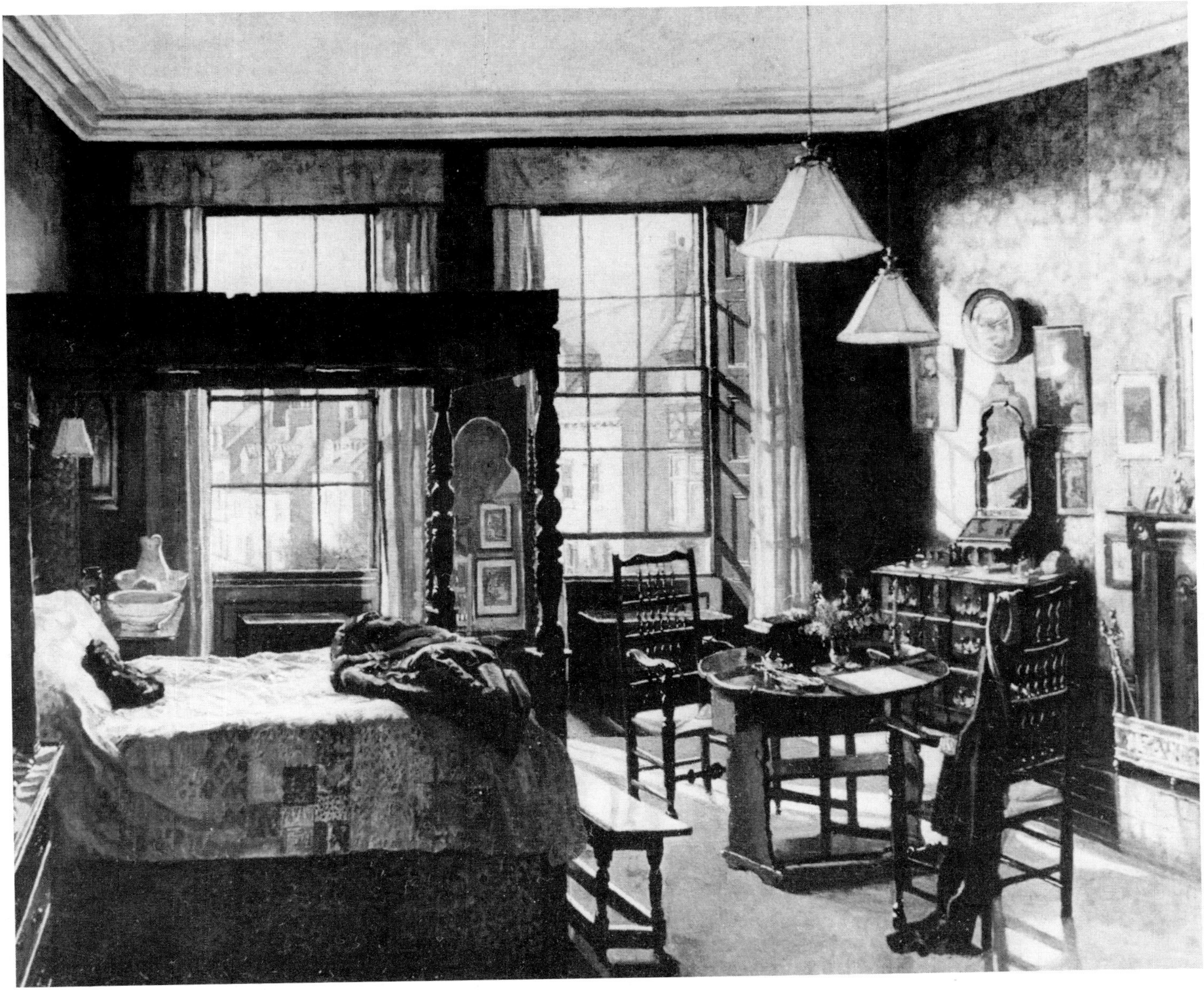

11. "The Bedroom in Summer" by Mary Dawson Elwell was exhibited at the Royal Academy in 1935 . North Bar Without can be seen through the window.

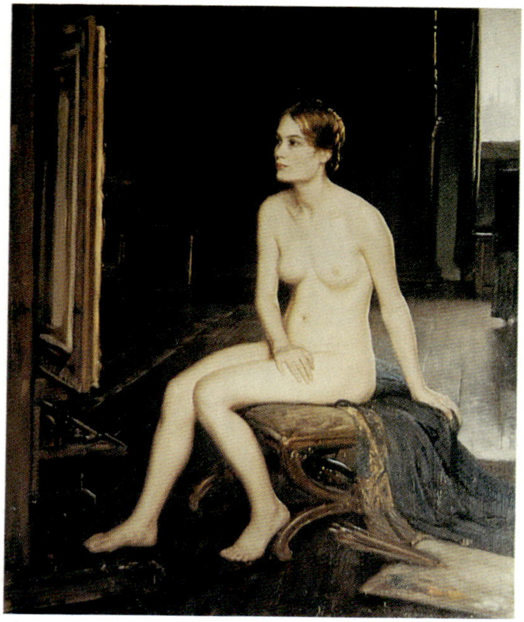

7. "The Artist's Model" was exhibited at the Royal Academyin 1935. Reproduced courtesy of Beverley Art Gallery.

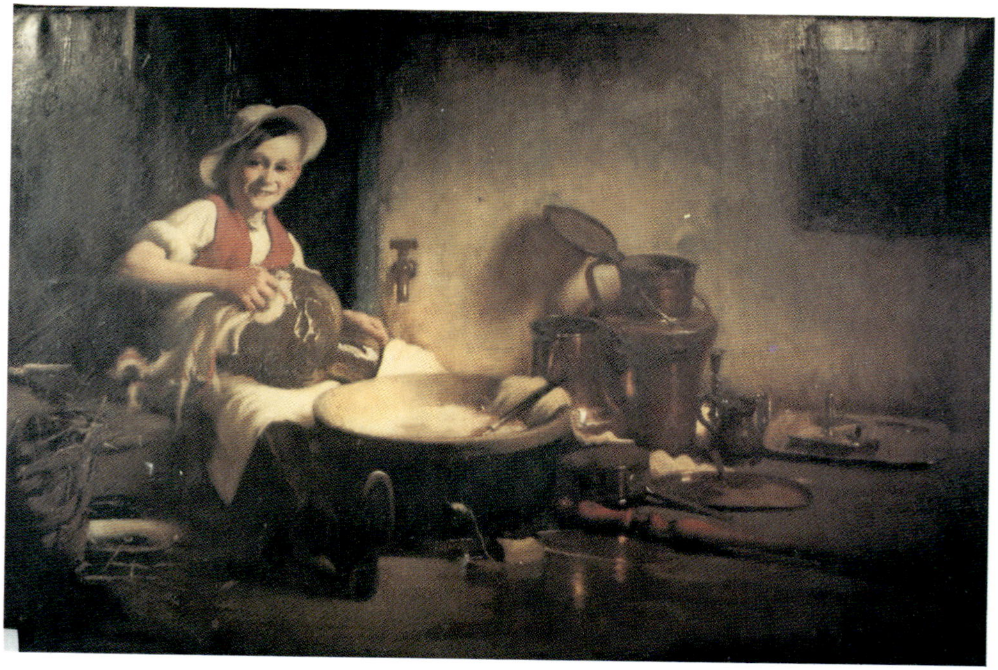

15. "The Pot Boy" (1903) sold at an auction in 1989 for £7,200. Picture by courtesy of Dee & Atkinson, Auctioneers, Driffield.

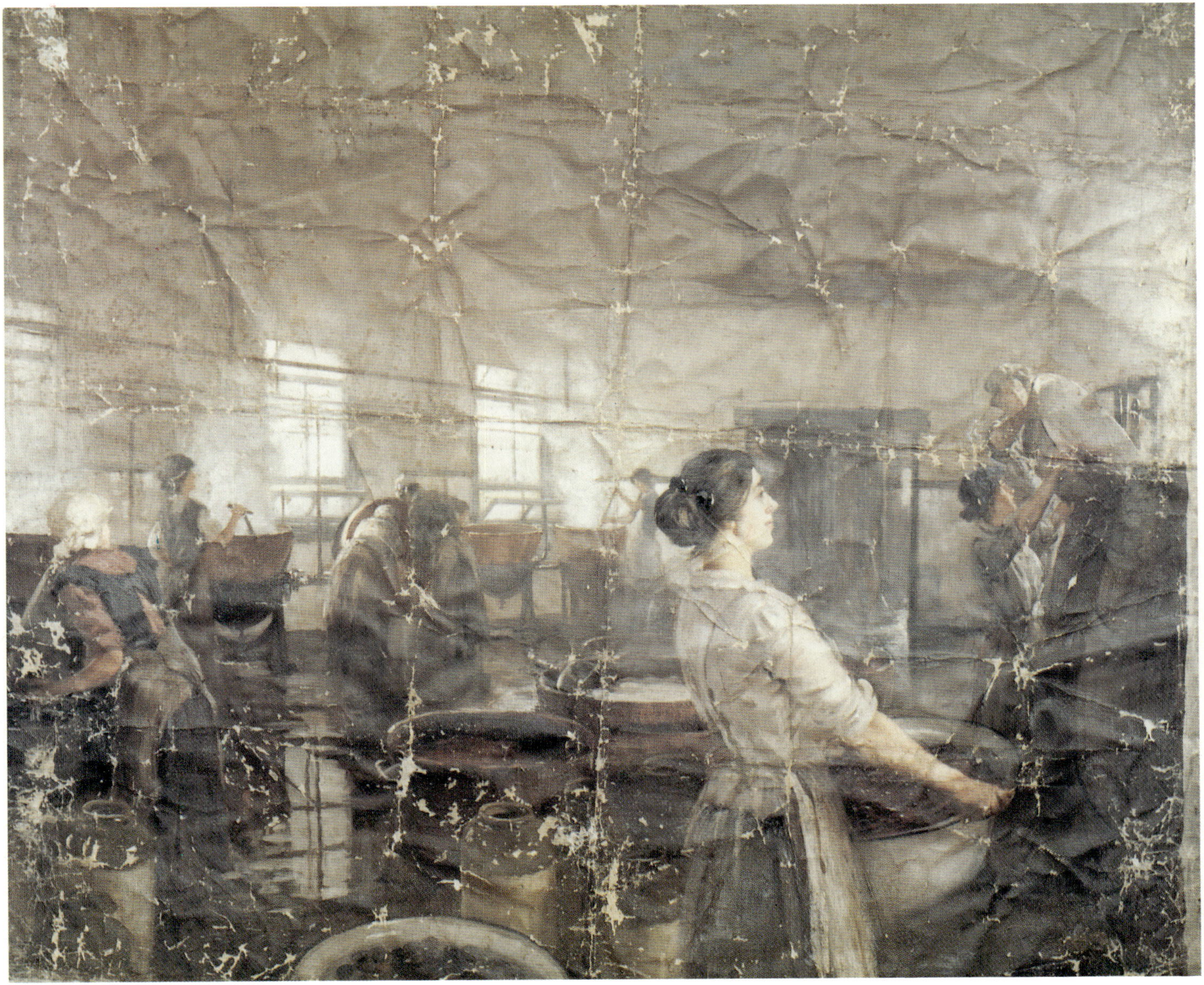

10. "The Driffield Jam Factory" was exhibited at the Royal Academy in 1918. This picture was found damaged in 1976, but was later restored (private collection).

has been re-named *Elwells* in honour of this tradition. Another favourite venue was the back of Abrams' cafe (now Hawley's antique shop). The friends would talk for about forty-five minutes, each buying their own drinks before going home for lunch, apart that is from Dickie Whiteing of Hengate House who went on to the White Horse in Hengate, otherwise known as Nellie's. Dickie Whiteing was well-known for his fondness for alcohol and on returning from a trip together, Fred was heard to remark, "I went in all the churches and Dickie into all the pubs, or was it the other way round?" and also "He's a dear friend, Dickie, but I wish he would keep himself cleaner".

Although the Beverley Arms was Fred's local, the Rose and Crown, just across the road from the Bar House, provided some of the wines and spirits for the house. At Bar House parties or at the Beverley Arms, when Fred was getting a round of drinks, a friend observed that he gave white wine to the ladies and red to the men. Only in his last year did he let everyone drink what they wanted.

On moving into the Bar House with Mamie, Fred now had a view of the *loveliest street in England* — North Bar Within. The house takes its name from the last remaining mediaeval gate or *bar* in Beverley, which it incorporates. Fred and Mamie liked to tell tales of the time when Charles I spent the night there. The Guardroom above the gateway had seventeenth and eighteenth century furniture. However, the family firm produced a small oak refectory table to suit the period. Mamie used this room as a studio, and painted many domestic interiors there (Fig.11).

Many rooms in the house were used as settings for pictures, including *The Last Purchase* (private), *The Window Seat* (private), *The Birthday Party* (Beverley Art Gallery) (Fig.12) and the *Housekeeper's Room* (Ferens Art Gallery, Hull).

The house was full of antiques, books and paintings. Every corner was crammed with cupboards, chairs, tables and bookcases which if sold today would raise thousands, but which at the sale of contents in 1958 went "for a song".

On entering, the visitor would be struck by the spaciousness of the hall with its dark oak furniture harmonising with the wide oak staircase carpeted in red. A beautiful bracket clock and longcase clock completed the scene. Mamie loved the effect of blue and white porcelain against dark oak and the old Welsh dresser in the dining room was full of this and decorated plates and pewter. In the drawing room, lit by a crystal chandelier, three large bookcases were bulging with books on travel, art, poetry, philosophy and gardening. The fireplace, designed by Richard Whiteing, resident architect at Beverley Minster, had an overmantle produced by James Elwell's company. A Meissen *Garniture de Cheminée* was a prized possession comprising two 3-branched rosebush candlesticks with delicate figures, plus a clock similarly entwined with a tracery of leaves and branches.

The majority of the paintings in the Bar House were by Fred and Mamie and friends, such as Richard Jack and Tom Bruce. A chalk drawing of Fred by Dame Laura Knight (Fig.13) is now in the Beverley Art Gallery and Sir Alfred Munnings' *Before the Flies Come* was sold at the Bar House sale in 1958 for £330.

One of the Jack's paintings was of the enclosed garden which also featured in many of Fred and Mamie's work, several of which are in the Beverley Art Gallery.

The acquisition of the house coincided with the surge in interest in gardening brought about to a certain extent by Gertrude Jekyll's books. Art training had given her an eye for colour and form in horticultural terms, as it had with Fred. Often working alongside his two gardeners, Fred particularly loved the rock garden. He would bring violets into the dining room and scatter them on the table set for dinner parties. Mr. J. Shaw, the rose grower, would bring rose bushes for the garden and this friendship led to the building up of the largest private Elwell collection.

To the front of the house is North Bar Within which Fred would show to guests asking, "Where could you find a lovelier street?" He recorded the view several times, perhaps most notably in the *Last Cab* (1931) (Beverley Art Gallery) for which the maid, Miss Doris Cooper, stood on a box in the studio posing with a wearily extended arm, later to be connected to a dog on a lead. Old Camm, the

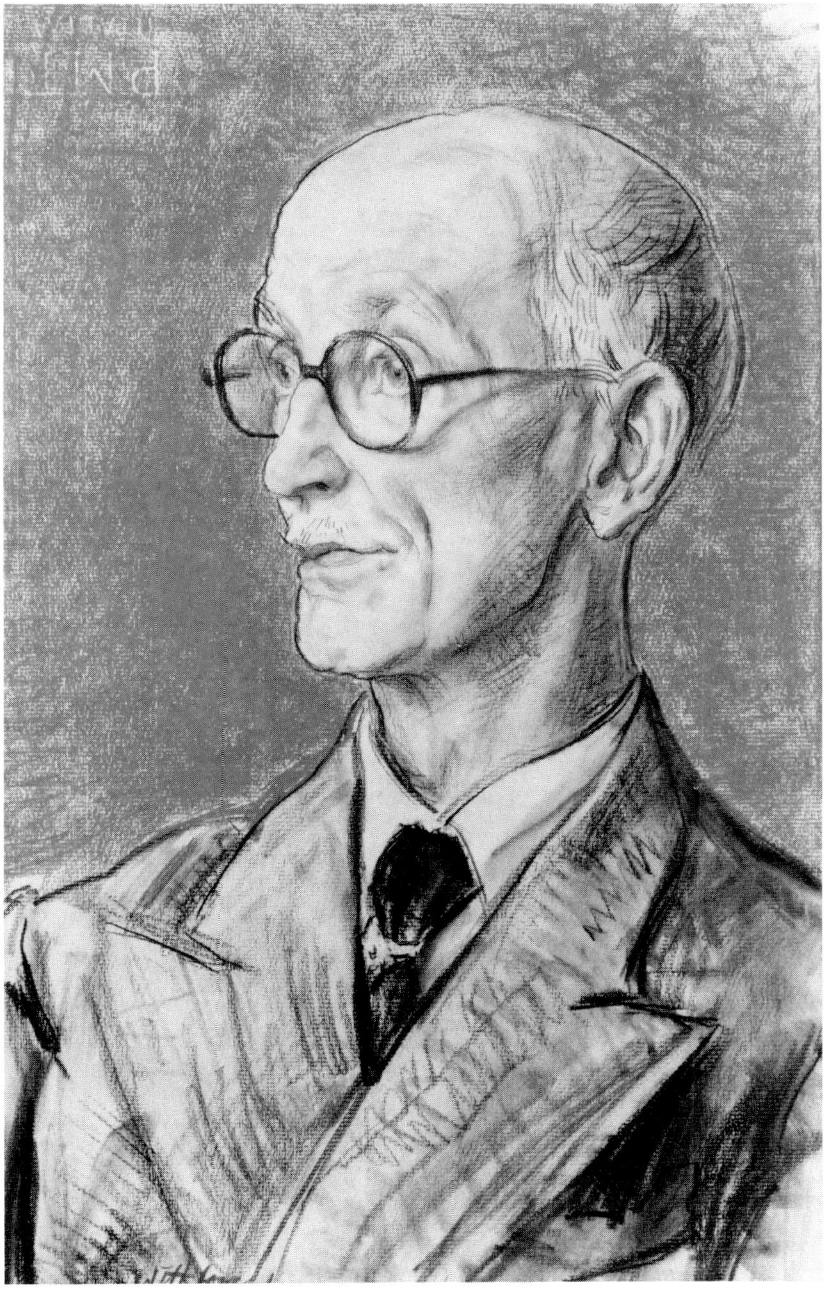

13. Dame Laura Knight's chalk drawing of Fred, now in Beverley Art Gallery. Reproduced courtesy of Beverley Art Gallery.

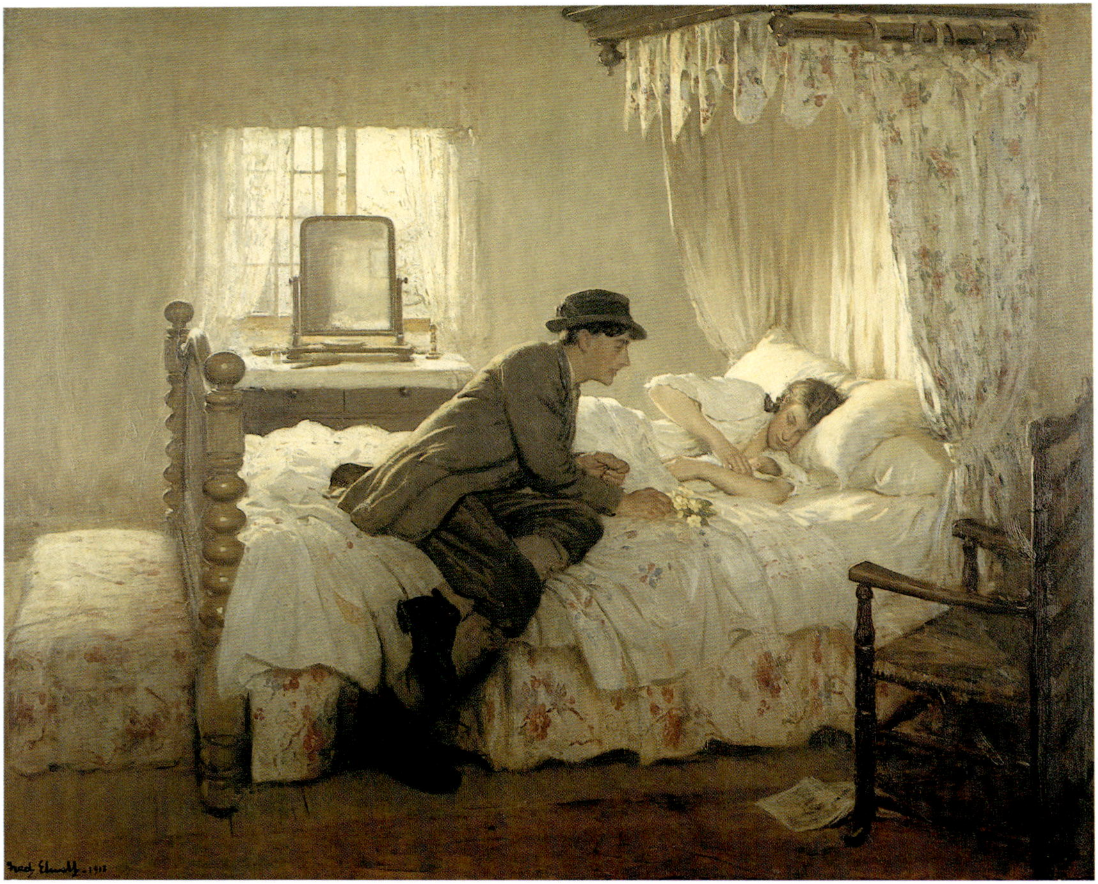

"The First Born" was exhibited at the Royal Academy in 1913. It is owned by the Ferens Art Gallery, Hull. Reproduced courtesy of Ferens Art Gallery: Hull City Museums & Art Galleries.

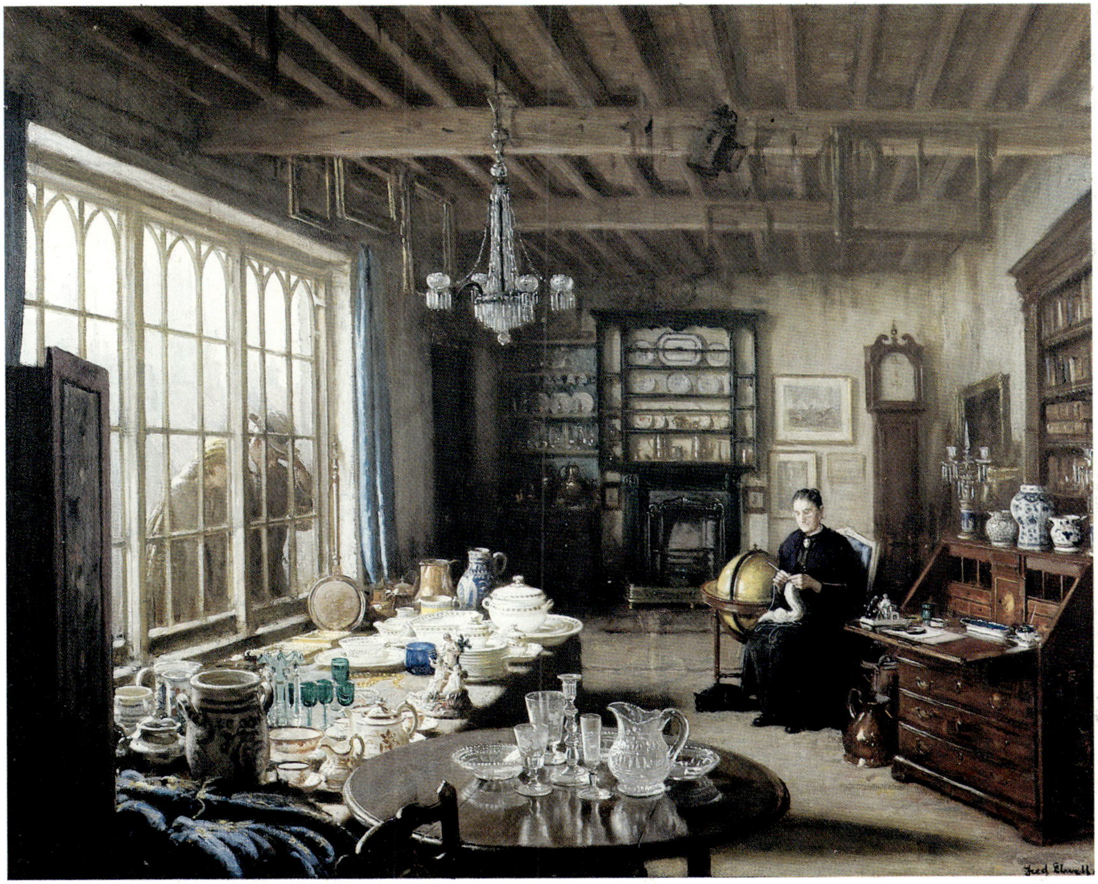

"The Curiosity Shop" was exhibited at the Royal Academy in 1930. Reproduced courtesy of the Harris Museum & Art Gallery, Preston.

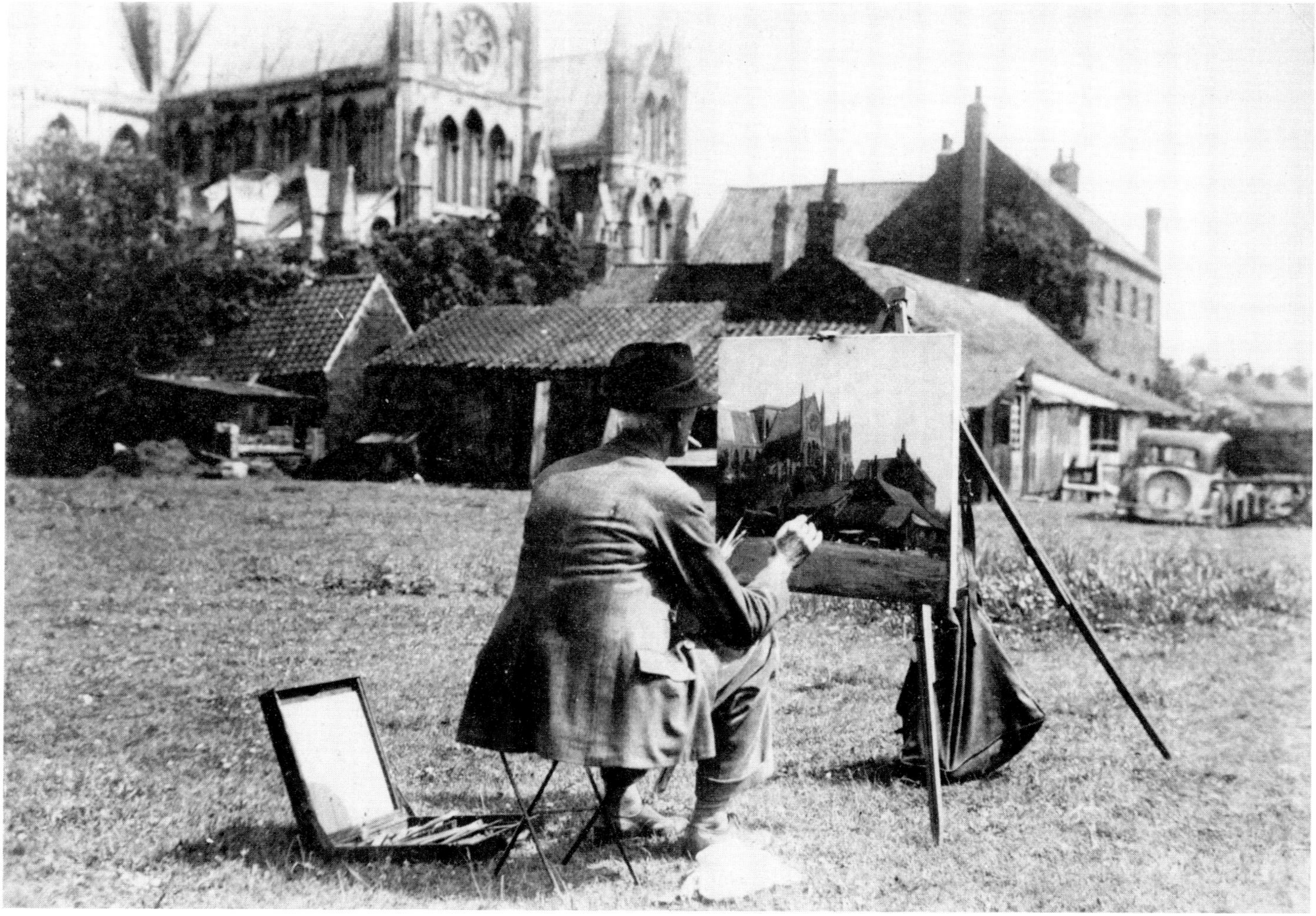

14. Photograph of Fred painting the Minster from Hall Garth. The painting was exhibited at the Royal Academy in 1943.

cabbie, waits for Mamie to alight from the cab. The cab was used to take the Elwells to and from the railway station to catch the train to Scarborough or London, via Hull. Local children played in the cab when kept at Miss Camm's school, Newbegin, in spite of it being used to take fever patients to hospital. The Elwells kept a Daimler, driven by chauffeur/gardener, Mr. Shaw. It was familiarly known as *Violet* and had a very low mileage which meant that it was quite a bargain for John "Lamorna" Birch, who purchased the last one from Fred.

On one occasion when returning from a trip in the Daimler, Fred saw an epileptic boy having a fit near the Bar House. He characteristically stopped the car and proffered help.

Always on the fringes and never a member of a group, Fred was naturally acquainted with members of the Newlyn and Staithes groups of artists. The French artist, Bastien-Lepage, had some influence in these groups. His impartial view of nature, as opposed to an *impression*, was combined with a profound respect for the dignity of the working man and found favour with artists like Gilbert Foster, Frederick Jackson and Harold Knight. Walter Sickert said that Bastien-Lepage was a *representative of that French tradition which has led inevitably to the sterile ideal of the instantaneous camera – the truth of inessentials.*

Fred was committed to representational art and expressed an admiration for François Millet about whom he once gave a lecture to Hull's Literary and Philosophical Society. Millet's quotation, "What you love with the greatest power and passion becomes the ideal of beauty which you impose on others," agrees with Fred's philosophy.

What Fred loved was his home town of Beverley. He painted lots of views of the street, the Minster (Fig.14) and the Beverley Arms which was the setting for *Elevenses*, *Girl Plucking a Goose*, *An Inn Kitchen*, *Three Maids*, *The Pot Boy* (Fig.15) and many more.

The Beverley Arms Kitchen was the Chantrey purchase from the artist in 1919 for the Tate Gallery. Under the Chantrey Bequest, left by Sir Francis Chantrey the Victorian sculptor, for creating a national art collection, the Academy bought pictures for the Tate Gallery. Unfortunately, the Tate trustees often refused to hang them until they were represented on the selection board in 1922. Fred's work was more in line with that likely to be approved of by the Royal Academy Establishment.

His paintings were generally well-liked, lending themselves to reproduction on calendars and in advertising. A local firm, Watts Brothers, used several one year on their calendar and a bedroom firm based a campaign on the *First Born*. An American company bought reproduction rights on *Silver and Gold*, a picture of the Beverley Brass Band. For this picture, Fred sat in on a practice in the bandroom at the King's Head in the Market Place. The band had been re-formed in May, 1918, with Mr. R. Cooper as bandmaster. Fred told the band that he could see a very beautiful picture forming as he sketched there and asked if they would practice in his studio for a few weeks. Later each member came individually to the studio to have his face added to the canvas, sometimes with arms propped up holding his instrument. The band received a new set of caps for their trouble.

Another unusual form of remuneration for modelling was a tea set given to a family whose dogs were the subject of a painting set in the yard of the house where the Clock Garage, Norwood, now stands.

The nearest thing Fred got to social comment was the R.A. picture of the year in 1933, *Man With a Pint*, when the Chancellor put a penny on the price of beer (Blackpool Art Gallery).

A genuine admiration for craftsmanship, handed down from his father, is shown in his workshop pictures. *The Last Pipemaker in Beverley* (1935) (Wilberforce House, Hull), *Widdalls* (1928) (Glasgow Art Gallery), *The Modelship Maker* (Fig.16) (Beverley Art Gallery) may signify the regret felt at the passing of an era unable to keep pace with technology. One of the pictures of the year in 1920, according to P.G. Konody in the London Observer

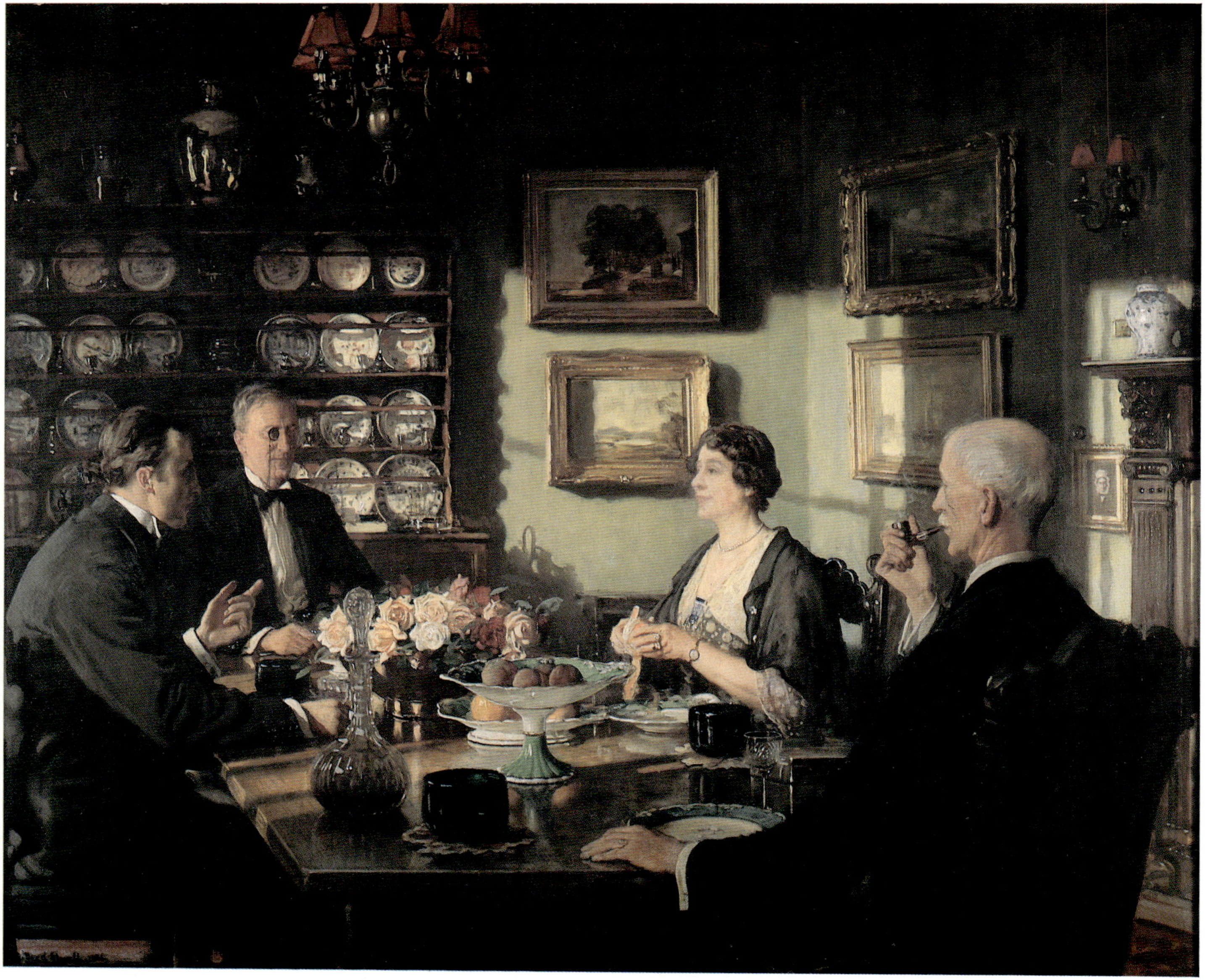

12. "The Birthday Party" (1936) hangs in Beverley Art Gallery. From left to right the guests are Kenneth Elwell, Richard Whiteing, Mary and Fred Elwell. Reproduced courtesy of Beverley Art Gallery.

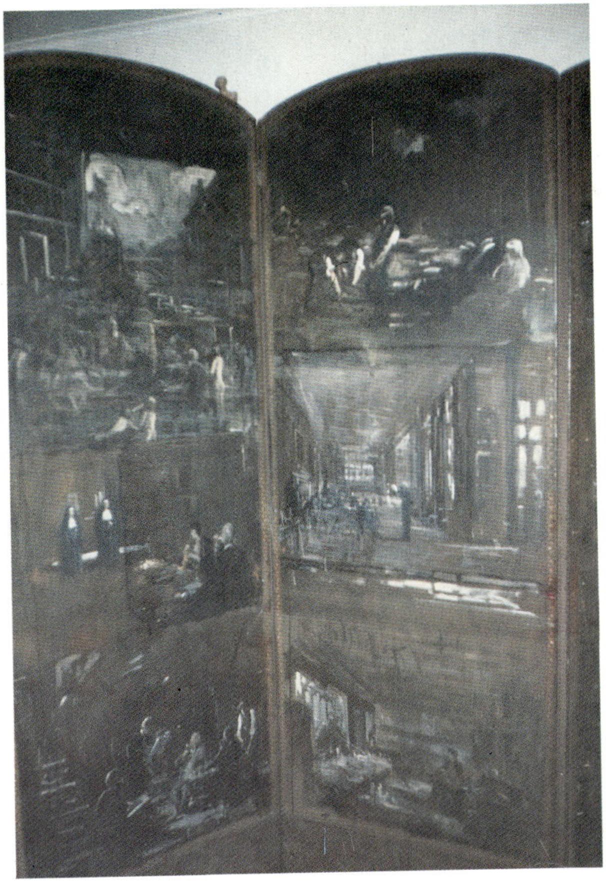

17. Screen with sketches from the 1930's and 1940's (private collection).

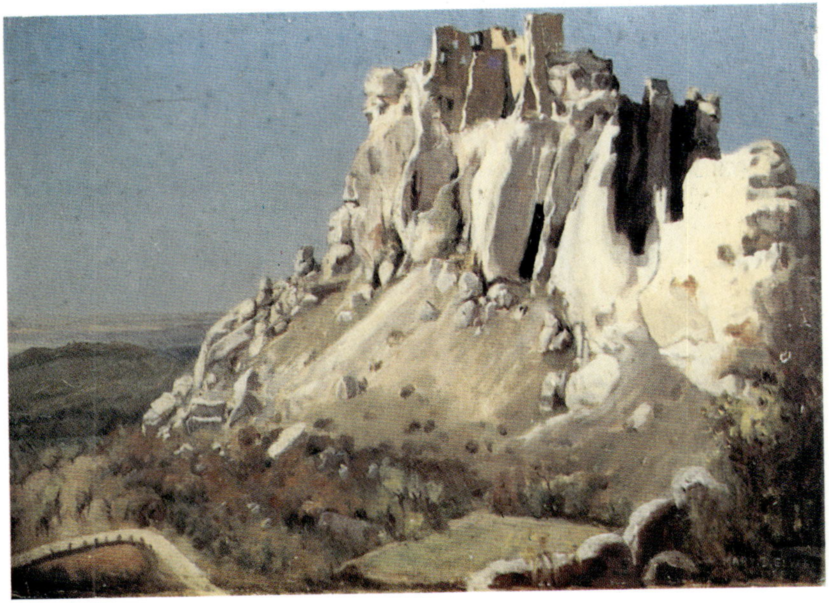

18. "Castle of Les Baux" (1928) by Mary Elwell. Photograph courtesy of Alison Balding.

was of James Elwell in the *Woodcarver's Shop — ...so far as competent craftsmanship and straightforward statement of facts are concerned, realism without blind acceptance of all accidents. The appearance of the accidental and of disorder kept up in a very carefully planned composition...*

Economically, Elwell used his backgrounds and props several times in different combinations to *make a picture*. The timbered roof of his Trinity Lane studio turns up in several interiors and a particular piece of blue and white pottery is an old favourite. Models too turn up over again: his father, wife and Fred himself, like Hitchcock in his own films, are present in various guises in many paintings. See them peering through the window in *The Curiosity Shop* (1930) (Back cover). In the *Window Seat*, the same model is used twice with a front and a back view. Family, friends and domestic staff were all called upon to sit. Any maid with a good pair of legs or profile was included; however the cook was omitted from *Morning Prayers* when Mamie said that her bottom was too big!

Fred would knock on doors in the area round his Trinity Lane studio to ask parents if their children would be willing to pose for him. Unfortunately when his back was turned, two juvenile models squeezed all the paint tubes into one lovely mess!

Careful line and tone were characteristics of the paintings and although he loved his work, there is little passion, the paint often being thinly applied with concealed brushstrokes, delineating form accurately, recording but not expressing. Over seventy years of painting he aimed for no more than to make a *beautiful picture* which is commendable in itself. Was Matisse thinking of such a man as Fred when he wrote ... *I am constantly amazed that some people can be so lacking in anxiety as to imagine that they have grasped the truth of their art on first try.*?

It can fairly be supposed that Fred did not have that anxiety. He painted what he wanted to paint. He aimed for a natural effect in his subject paintings but his portraits were generally classically posed, half-length figures. Many local businessmen and civic dignitaries and their wives sat for Fred: Frederick Needler, Alderman Harry Wray, John Champney, Thomas Hudson J.P., the Rt. Hon. T.R. Ferens, Sir Prince Prince-Smith, Lt. Col. Raleigh Chichester Constable and many more.

Not all his patrons were completely satisfied however. When the shareholders and directors of Horsley Smith & Co. Ltd., commissioned a seventieth birthday portrait of Alexander Alec-Smith O.B.E. in 1947, the cost was £273. A few years later when the family tried to buy a discarded oil sketch of the subject, done at the same time, Fred asked for a further fifty guineas which led to some heated correspondence. The family did eventually acquire the picture.

Fred worked up his large paintings from several oil sketches, some of which were framed and given to friends and relations as gifts. He prepared all his own canvasses, generally wearing his trilby to shield his eyes when working. Some initial white oil sketches on a dark background can be seen on two folding screens. One of these, owned by the Beverley Art Circle and now in Beverley Art Gallery, has scenes in the Bar House garden, and sketches for the *New Frock*, *The First Born*, *The Cowshed*, *Refugees* and several more can be identified. The other screen (Fig.17) which is in private hands has sketches for the *Window Seat*, *Brick Bridge*, *Swinemoor*, *The Last Cab*, *Girl Plucking a Goose*, *Reading of the Will*, *Morning Prayers*, *Arden's Vaults* and the *Old Curiosity Shop*. Also on the screen are sketches of Fred's nephew, Kenneth Elwell, himself no mean artist, specialising in portraits, landscapes and hunting scenes.

Kenneth painted several pub signs including one for the Woolpack Inn on Westwood Road, replaced in 1989 by a modern one. Visitors to Trinity Lane were accustomed to being admitted by Ken wearing a variety of costumes as he modelled for his uncle. Sadly he was killed during the Second World War.

The First Born (Frontispiece), exhibited at the Royal Academy in 1913 and now owned by the Ferens Art Gallery in Hull, was tried out in several ways — on the screen and in oil sketches. *Slumber* exhibited in 1914 is a

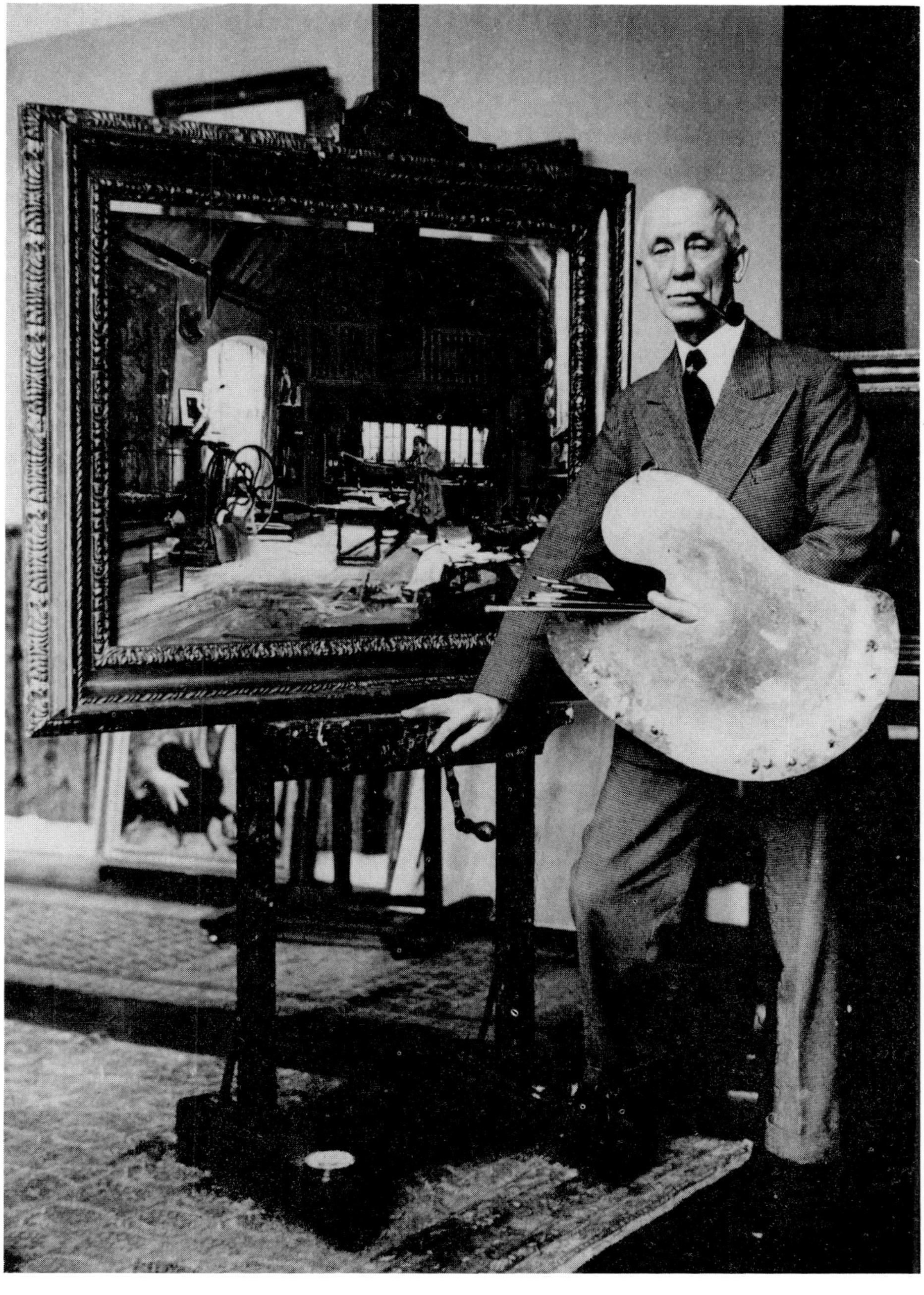

16. Photograph of Fred with his "Model Ship Builder", now in Beverley Art Gallery.

painting of a sleeping woman in a setting very similar to that of *The First Born* and probably developed from the same source. There are several claimants for the rôle of the adult models, but the baby is Mrs. Muriel Holtby, who said that Fred waited for her to be born in March, 1913 to complete the picture and spent two hours painting her head. She got 2/6d. for posing, quite a sum in a family where the policeman father earned 22/4½d. per week! The husband is generally thought to be a joiner who was killed when he fell from a gantry at the racecourse grandstand. Apparently there were heated arguments about whether the man should be wearing a hat. Fred insisted however that in his haste to see the baby, he would not have removed it. Several prints signed by Fred are in existence. It is an emotional picture, the paint more thickly applied than many of his. Typically, the light from a window and an unseen source spills warm pink tones over the carefully painted forms. Perhaps in this year before his marriage, Fred was in a particularly romantic mood, maybe hoping for a family himself, although Mamie was forty when they married.

All the nephews and nieces were welcome at the Bar House, and Fred paid the school fees of several of his nephews and great-nephews. Some of the younger members of the family were in awe of Mamie and the succession of chows which she kept, noted for nipping unwary ankles under the table. However distant she appeared to strangers, Mamie could still laugh when Fred said her trees looked like brussel sprouts!

When many households were getting mechanised and reducing staff, the Elwells employed about five indoor staff and two gardeners. Mamie insisted on a high degree of cleanliness, without the aid of a vacuum cleaner; all the carpets were beaten in the back garden. The housekeeper did in fact threaten to leave unless they invested in a vacuum cleaner. The cook ensured a plentiful supply of freshly-baked cakes and bread. There were no shop-bought pastries. Tame pigeons would come to the kitchen window to be fed, providing another title — *Maids With Pigeons* (1918).

Traditional spring-cleaning time saw Fred and Mamie leaving for Europe, not returning until a postcard from the housekeeper gave them the all-clear.

The Elwells loved to travel and had a wide collection of travel books covering Italy, Greece, Belgium and Spain as well as Britain. They painted and sketched together, especially in Italy and France. Their favourite places in France were Albi, Cahors and Les Baux, wine-growing areas where Fred cultivated his taste for red wine. Les Baux is a half-mile long bare rock spur with vertical ravines on either side. The village is only accessible on foot and it really impressed the pair as they painted it at different times of the day and in different light conditions, trying to capture its magical quality (Fig.18). The area is not far from Van Gogh's Arles but there can scarcely be a greater contrast in response to an area.

In Britain, *Violet* the Daimler took them around great country houses in order to complete commissions and to visit their many friends. Domestic interiors were commissioned at Glamis Castle, Eaton Hall, Thorpe Hall, Castle Ashby, Burton Constable Hall, and Compton Court, Somerset, plus many more. Personal recommendation was the source of many commissions.

For a summer season in the 1920's, Fred and Mary lived in a caravan, travelling around with Sanger's Circus. Initially, the circus management were not too keen on Fred's project but agreed on condition that his horse-drawn caravan would be last in the procession except for the farrier. This was so that any breakdown would not impede the rest of the cavalcade as it went from town to town. It was a source of pride to Fred that they had trouble with neither horse nor caravan throughout the summer. When it had become known in Beverley that the Elwells were in need of a horse, they were besieged by equines in all possible conditions and had to get Captain Storey, a local expert, to make a selection for them. The caravan was put to good use after the trip, as a changing room at the tennis club after the pavilion had burned down. *Horse Tent* (Fig.19), *Circus Horses*, *The Big Top*, *The Circus Forge*, *An Afternoon Performance* and *Performers' Entrance* were all painted at this time and several are in the Beverley Art Gallery.

Along with many contemporary artists, Fred was asked to contribute a miniature painting for Queen Mary's Doll's House and he decided that a circus picture would be the most suitable.

In 1935, with a studio in Holland Park, London, and owning three other houses in Beverley, the Elwells were really enjoying life. Mamie did most of the business side, writing letters and arranging appointments and commissions. She devoted herself to making Fred's life as harmonious and pleasant as possible. She believed that Fred was under-estimated in the East Riding and enjoyed the company of other artists centred in London. There were agreeable and stimulating friends, house-parties, dinner parties and fancy-dress parties. Fred did not always dress up at these events but did once put a towel over his arm and played the part of a waiter, and when a woman friend arrived as a Christmas pudding he was heard to observe that he was glad she wasn't a tart!

Wednesdays meant bridge parties for Mamie and other Masonic *widows* during Lodge meetings. There were garden parties at the Bar House which attracted all the *County*. One, in May, 1926, was opened by Liberal candidate Neville Dixey in aid of party funds. The garden was filled with money-raising stalls and even a brass band. Every year a garden party would be held in aid of Dr. Barnardo's Homes, the inspiration for yet another painting.

Sir Alfred Munnings stayed at the Bar House several times attending Beverley Races and on summer painting expeditions he painted horses whilst *dear old Fred* painted pigs, sometimes trying to ride them! *The Evening Meal* (Beverley Art Gallery) and *Pigs in a Barn*, a "cathedral-like barn near Newmarket", was sold to Nottingham Art Gallery for £210 in 1944. A wonderful picture of a boy holding a pig, painted in 1935, hangs in Blackpool's Grundy Art Gallery. Several porcine models were from Mr. Cook's Mount Pleasant Farm, Bishop Burton.

At the British Empire Exhibition, the Prince of Wales noticed an Elwell painting of *Girls in Needler's Dining Room* and expressed a wish to see some more of Hull's industries. On 19th May, 1926, the Prince laid the foundation stone of the Ferens Art Gallery, Hull and went on to visit Needler's confectionery factory, Sissons paint factory and the National Radiator Company, and stayed at Hotham Hall the home of Lt. Col. Stracey-Clitherow.

Fred regularly journeyed to London for Varnishing Days at the Royal Academy or to attend one of the four dinners a year held by the dining club in the Reynolds Room, beginning with a whitebait feast in May. He stayed at the Redbourne Hotel or the Dover Street Arts Club which had a table reserved for Royal Academicians. He was a member of the Chelsea Art Club where he met up with Reggie Brundritt, Harold Knight and John "Lamorna" Birch. Fred was known for his gentle charm, sense of fun, personal kindness and exquisite clothes. He said that it cost him a lot of money in entertaining other Academicians to successfully establish himself, and on 24th April 1931 Fred became an A.R.A. His certificate hangs in Lincoln College of Art.

Later that year King George V admired a portrait of Lt. Col. J.B. Stracey-Clitherow at the Royal Academy. This was thought by Mamie to be one of Fred's best, and very soon Fred was called to London to discuss arrangements for a portrait of the King (Fig.20). They got on famously. His Majesty sat several times for the painting with both of them chain-smoking. In order to complete it, the robes of the Order of the Thistle were brought to Trinity Lane Studio in great secrecy, guarded at night by Kenneth Elwell. The painting now hangs in the throne-room at Holyrood Palace and a first sketch of it is in the Beverley Art Gallery.

Soon after this, the tenants of the Earl and Countess of Strathmore and Kinghorne, parents of the Queen Mother, commissioned a painting to celebrate their Golden Wedding. The Earl is captured leaning against the mantlepiece, the Countess sitting on a sofa. Whilst there Fred painted an interior of a small drawing-room, undaunted by the reported presence of two ghosts, and

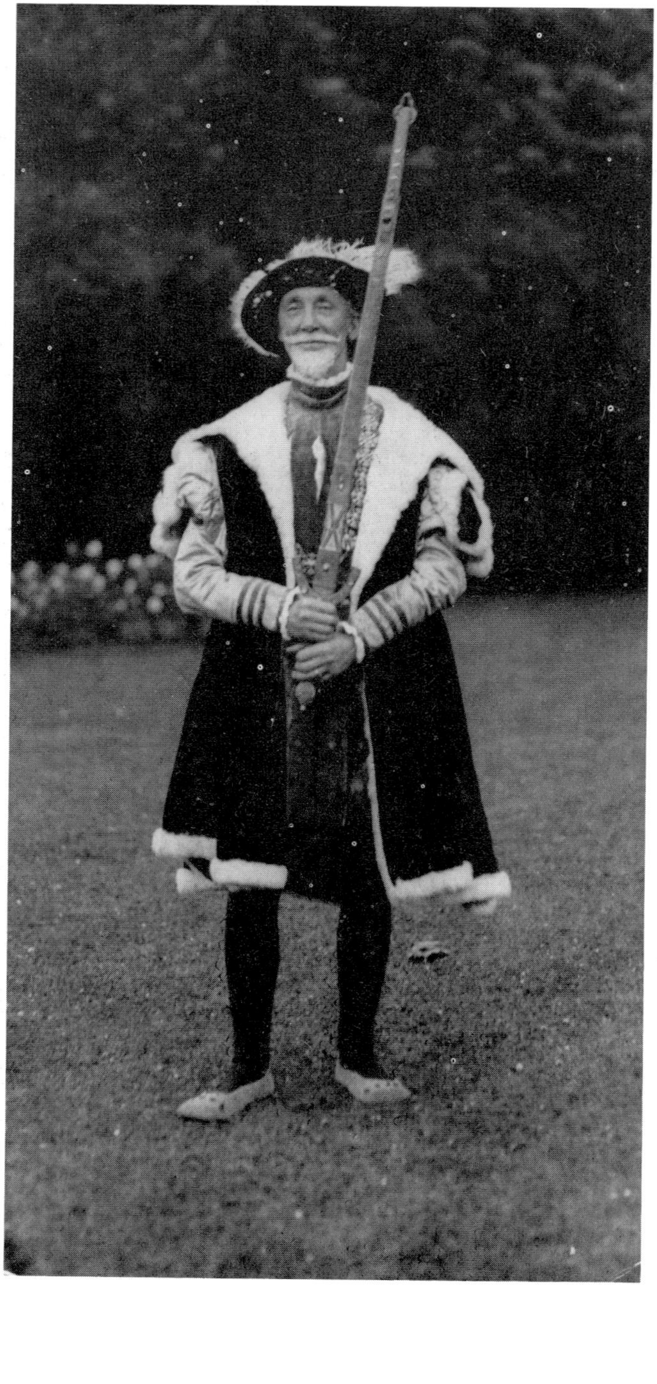

21. Photograph of Fred as the Earl of Hastings in the Pageant "Beverley Through the Ages" (1937). Reproduced courtesy of Peter Robinson.

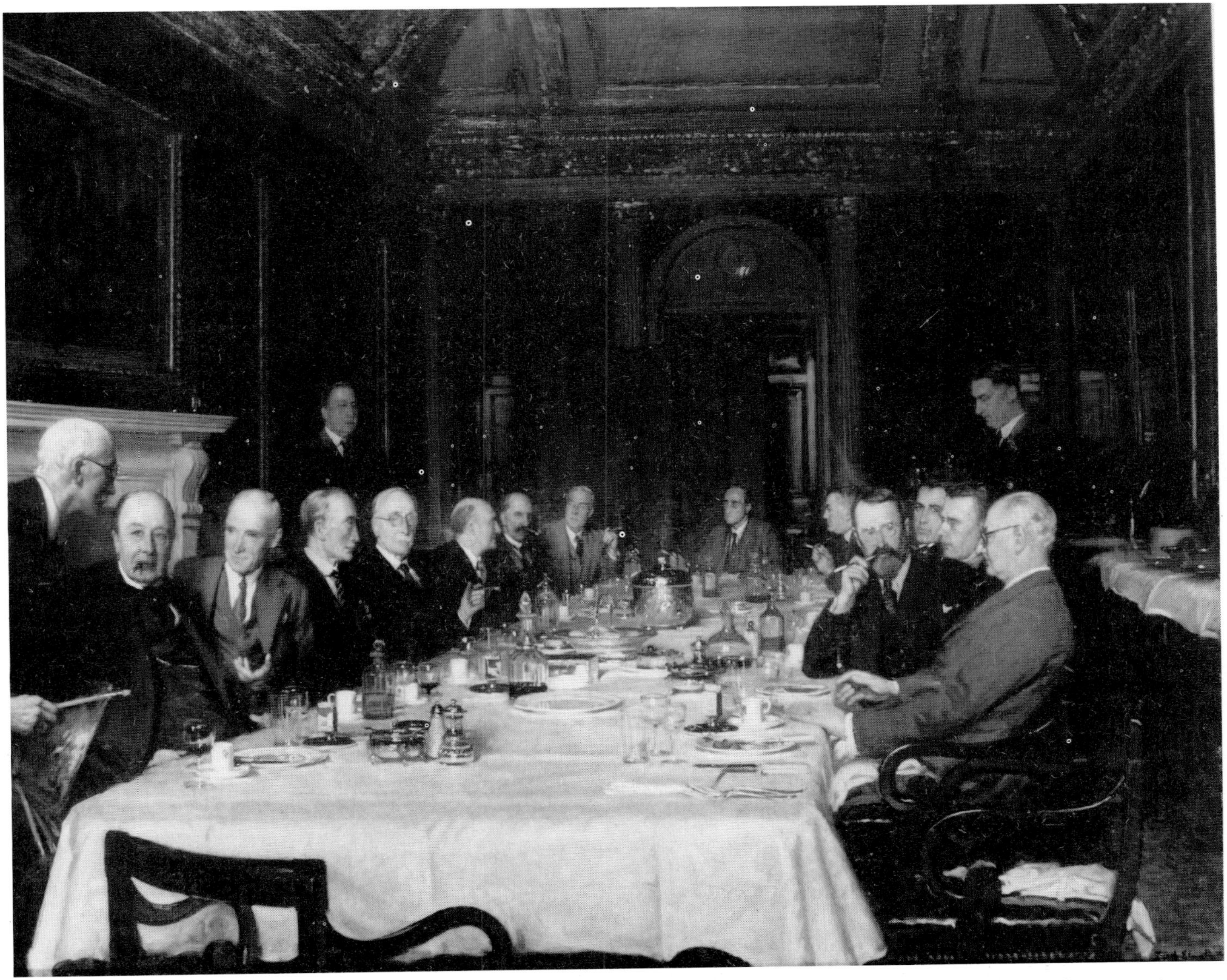

22. "The R.A. Selection & Hanging Committee" was Fred's diploma work when he was elected to become a Royal Academician in 1939. Reproduced courtesy of the Royal Academy.

presented it to the Queen Mother who told him in a delightful letter that ... *you have caught the atmosphere perfectly*.

Although never particularly welcoming people watching him working and not always sympathetic to amateurs, Fred accepted an invitation to give a painting demonstration to Huddersfield Art Society in 1935. He was said to be very nervous, but in one and a half hours produced a good painting of the Society's secretary at his easel.

Annually, Fred invited friends and relations to the house or studio to see the paintings which he was sending down to the Summer Exhibition, usually via Watts Bros., a haulage firm. On one occasion, a boy model for *An Artist's Heaven* observed that he did not like a man's hand in the picture. Despite being hushed by his mother, Fred overheard and said that the boy was quite correct and altered the offending hand. Another example of Fred's modesty came when he gave a flower painting to a friend saying deprecatingly, "Anyway, the frame's a good one!"

Fred and Mamie were fond of the theatre and the cinema. When *Lease of Life* was being shot on location at Beverley (Gilchester in the film) in 1954 with Robert Donat, co-star Adrienne Corri came to lunch at the Bar House. Fred actually took part in a film made by Ernest Symmons of the Playhouse Cinema in Beverley. In 1937, *Beverley Through the Ages* saw Fred playing the Earl of Hastings (Fig.21) and acquitting himself very well in a twenty minute recording of the pageant through Beverley to celebrate the Coronation. The festivities included the *Miss Beverley* competition. Fred was asked to propose the toast to Miss Beverley, 1936 — Mary Austin, and declared "The Queen is dead, long live the Queen! However Miss Austin is far from dead and I hope to have a dance with her later".

Fred was a popular after dinner speaker, never appearing to prepare speeches but loving to entertain his audience with any stories that strayed through his mind about his past life. He often spoke at Rotary lunches held at the Beverley Arms on Fridays.

At the age of 68, Fred became a Royal Academician. His diploma work, *The R.A. Selection and Hanging Committee, 1938* is fascinating in its detail and meticulous portraits. From left to right they are: Fred, Sir Edwin Cooper, Sir William Russell Flint, Sydney Lee, Sir William Llewellyn (President), Sir Walter Lamb (Secretary), Oliver Hall, George Harcourt, Sir Walter Russell, James Woodford, Stephen Gooden, Gilbert Ledward, John "Lamorna" Birch and Harold Knight (Fig.22).

Fred was too old for service in either of the World Wars. However, his wartime paintings have all the positive aspects of Government posters aiming to boost morale, portraying work going on in munitions and jam factories (Fig.10). His 1944 *Wheelwrights Shop* (Fig.23) (Beverley Art Gallery) painted at Thompson's workshop near the shipyard, includes black market ham shanks (never actually there of course) and a *Family Scene* could easily be an official warning on the evils of wasting food. Several pictures were destroyed in the Blitz when Hammonds furniture repository in Hull was bombed.

A happier time was recorded in 1943 on a hot summer day on Swinemoor when the *Brick Bridge Bathing Pool* (Beverley Art Gallery) was the place to be. Several Beverlonians recall the artist sketching among crowds of splashing children enjoying the only holiday excursion some of them ever experienced.

The fanciful title *I Dreamt St. Peter Sat for His Portrait*, exhibited at the R.A. in 1947, is a painting of George Bernard Shaw, whom, Fred probably met at one of Barry Jackson's Malvern House parties. When Augustus John painted G.B.S., he had to wait for him to fall asleep for him to stop talking. Undoubtedly with Fred's famed loquacity there must have been some great debates. Fred's fee for a portrait around this time was 250 guineas.

Fred seemed tireless in his work and at the age of 76, took on the enormous task of portraying *A Luncheon to Celebate the 500th Anniversay of the Shrievalty of Kingston-upon-Hull* (Fig.24) which hangs in Hull's Guildhall, and includes over fifty portraits, including that of Winston Churchill, Sheriff R.G. Tarran, Capt. George Fox, Sir

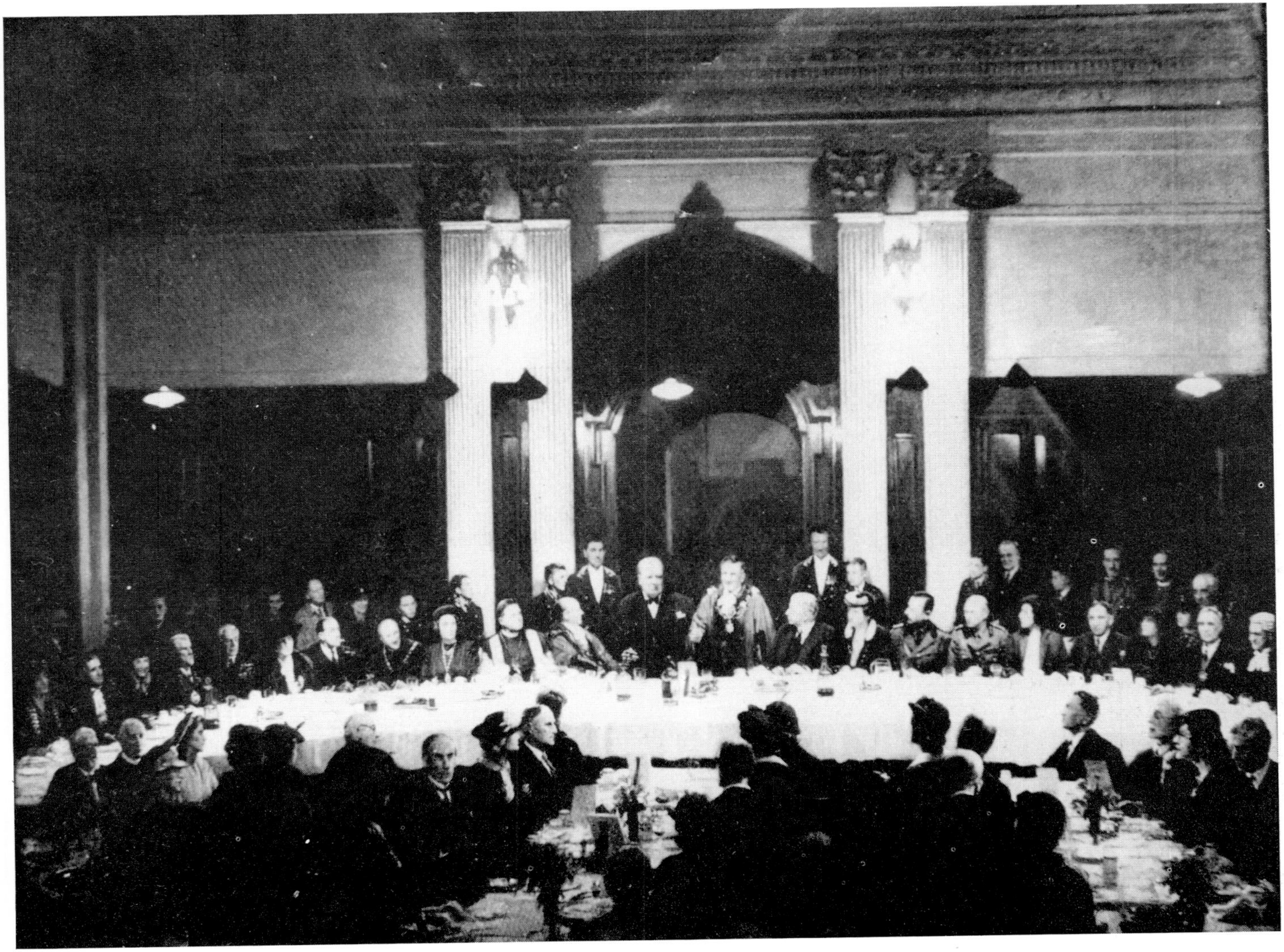

24. *"A Sheriff's Luncheon" hangs in Hull's Guildhall and celebrates the visit of Winston Churchill to the city in 1946. Reproduced courtesy of Hull City Council.*

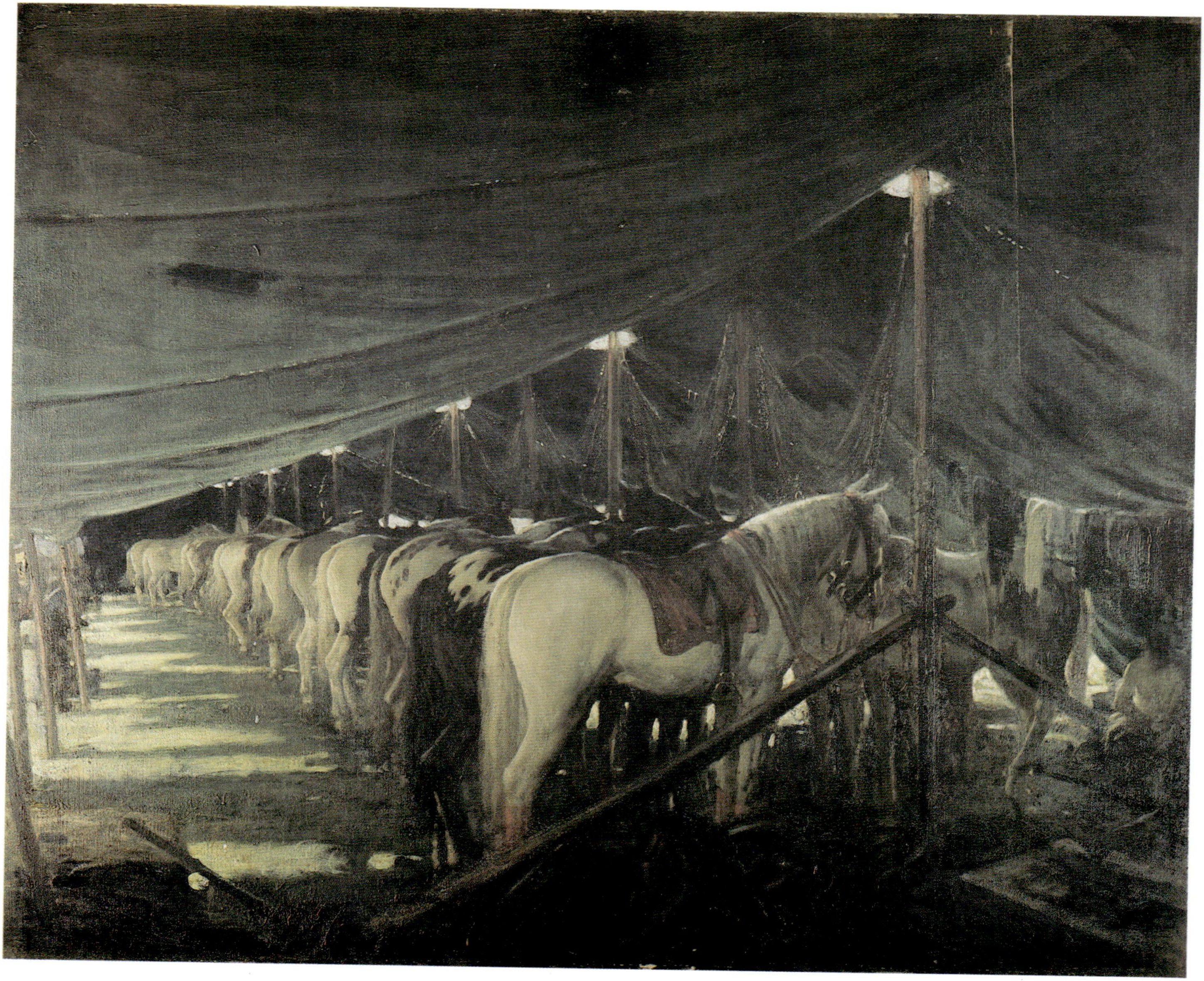

19. "The Horse Tent" was painted when Fred and Mary travelled around with Sanger's Circus in 1923. Reproduced courtesy of Beverley Art Gallery.

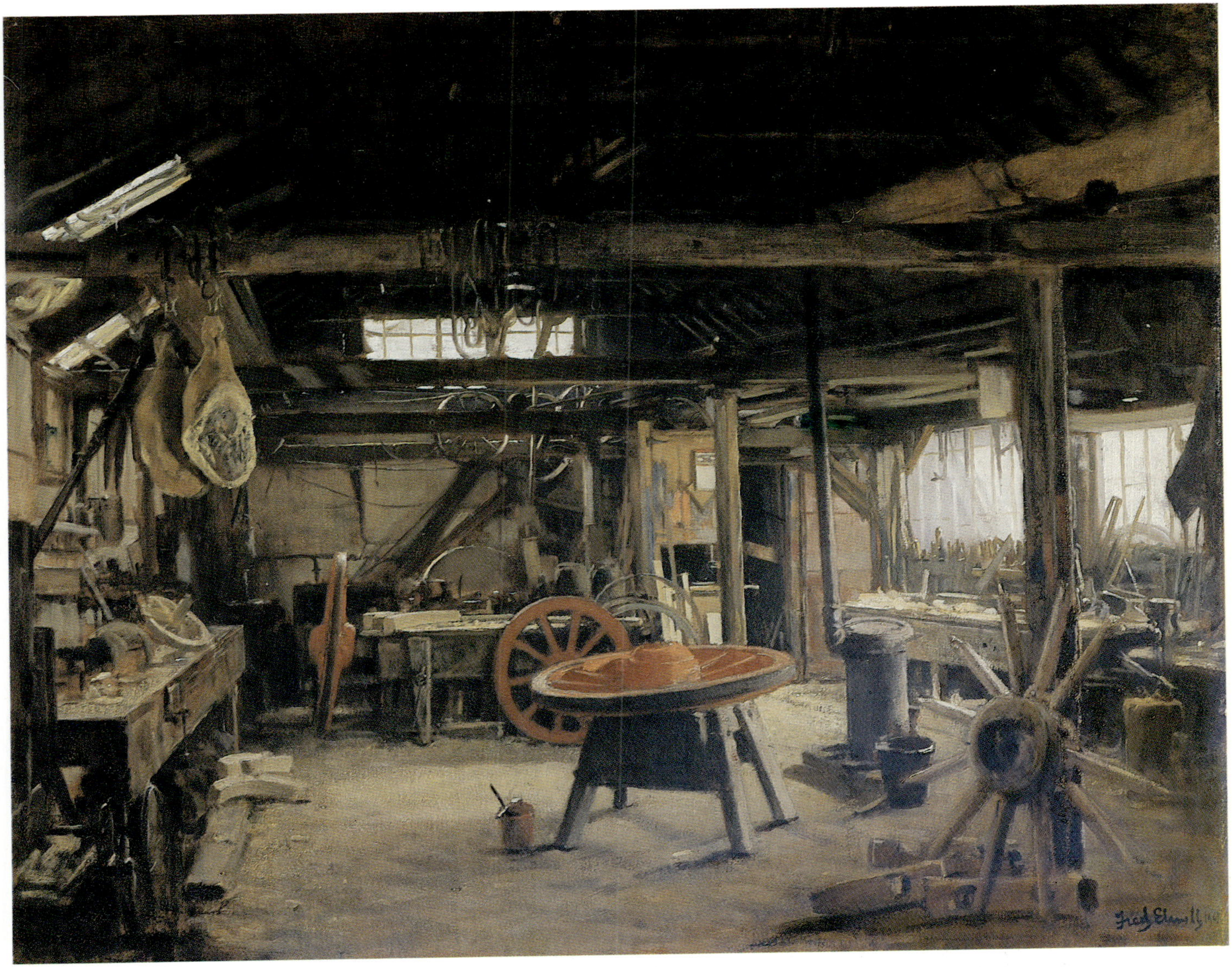

23. "The Wheelwright's Shop" was exhibited at the Royal Academy in 1945. The killing of the pigs and the hanging of the hocks had obviously been done surreptitiously during war-time strictures. Reproduced courtesy of Beverley Art Gallery.

Arthur and Lady Atkinson, and Fred and Mamie in the bottom right-hand corner.

Bohemian by Beverley standards, Fred Elwell was a very well-known figure with his black velour hat and patterned scarf (usually a remnant from the Saturday Market) (Fig.25), around his neck and threaded through his father's gold ring. The ring had the inscription *Mary Wilkinson died 6th June, 1776* and is clearly shown on his father's hand in the *Last Purchase* (Fig.3).

Like his father, Fred took an active part in the life of the town. As a J.P. he reckoned that he used his artistic judgement of the accused's face to reach a verdict. He was on the committee of the East Riding Antiquarians, dedicated to preserving old buildings.

One young Beverley man went to see the Summer Exhibition in 1948 and stood admiring Elwell's *Geraniums*. He fell into conversation with a woman remarking that he knew the artist. Friendship blossomed, they married two years later and red geraniums flourished annually in their garden. When they looked at the flowers, Mr. and Mrs. Rounthwaite always had fond memories of the artist who had brought them together.

In 1952, Mary Elwell died after a long illness, a stroke having robbed her of the power of speech. A generous if self-effacing woman, she was a good artist in her own right, exhibiting 58 paintings at the Royal Academy over 22 years. She regarded her interiors and landscapes as a hobby and had to be prevailed upon to sell them. She gave money for the extension to the Cottage Hospital in Beverley and laid the foundation stone in 1935. The Beverley Boys' Club and the Church had reason to be grateful for her generosity.

Although lonely after Mamie's death, Fred was amazingly sprightly and in 1953 was made an Honorary Freeman of Beverley. After a dinner of pheasant and peach melba, the Mayor, P.D. Dunn, said, "In the innermost heart of this casket, secure there forever are the goodwill and homage of your fellow townsmen".

In the same year, an exhibition of Fred and Mary's works was held in Beverley Art Gallery to celebrate the Coronation. Fred's appetite for work had not diminished and a portrait of Elizabeth Chapman, his housekeeper, was still wet when it went on show. He told a reporter, "It's not so bad for over eighty is it?"

After many years of supporting and judging arts and crafts shows, Fred instigated the foundation of the Beverley and District Arts Club in 1955. The Group met in rooms over Greens (now Fletchers) in Saturday Market. In his speech at the opening he said how he deplored the tendency of modern painters to "just dash it off. Just dashing things off does not lead to anything. Every picture you do you should try and make better than the one you did before". When asked to be president he said, "Well I am president of another club and do nothing for them and so I'll do just the same for you".

He did not involve himself in the running of the club, but turned up occasionally, encouraging, advising and setting subjects. For example, one week he proposed *A Storm* and then a *Picnic* neither of which were typical Elwell subjects. He gave money for heaters and at Christmas gave the group a party and a big ham. He assembled the annual exhibition himself, never omitting the paintings of anyone who had tried.

Fred kept painting until shortly before his death. Flower studies and old themes were obviously easier for him then. There were two paintings exhibited posthumously at the Academy in 1958. *Craigbulg Castle Keep* sold for £125 and the *Pickwick Club* for £150.

On 3rd January 1958, Fred died. Although he claimed to belong to no religion, and would not have objected to a Mohammedan funeral, he even-handedly left £250 to both the Minster and to St. Mary's Church, plus £500 to the Church Lads' Brigade.

Fred and Mamie's gravestone is in St. Mary's churchyard just through the gate. At the top of the portland stone memorial is a panel upon which, according to Fred's directions, Mr. K. Pape, the local monumental mason, carved an easel, brushes, paints and palette.

The Bar House was sold for £2,400 and after being a private residence for many years, became an art gallery and is now offices.

A fascinating postcript to Fred Elwell's story has been the discovery in 1976 of a pile of discarded canvasses on the floor of the studio in Trinity Lane (Fig.26). Edward Elwell, Fred's nephew, had used the ground floor for furniture-making whilst Fred painted upstairs. However as Fred got too old to climb the stairs, he gave it up and the place was abandoned until a local firm wished to use it as a warehouse. Some very early work was found and has now been restored including *Le Lendemain de la Mi Carême* (Fig.8) or the *Day After the Fête* which had been exhibited in Paris. This depicts a girl at a laundry table, confetti on the floor, gazing forlornly at a carnival poster, whilst her fellow-workers get on with the ironing. Also revealed were a *Knife-Grinder*, *A Violinist*, *A Jam Factory* (Fig.10), *A Ship on the Stocks* and *A Nude in a Cave*, as well as several oil sketches.

Although Fred's popularity as an artist ebbed and flowed during his long career, his undoubted talent and his manifest enjoyment of his work survives and undoubtedly Beverley can be proud of its Elwell connection.

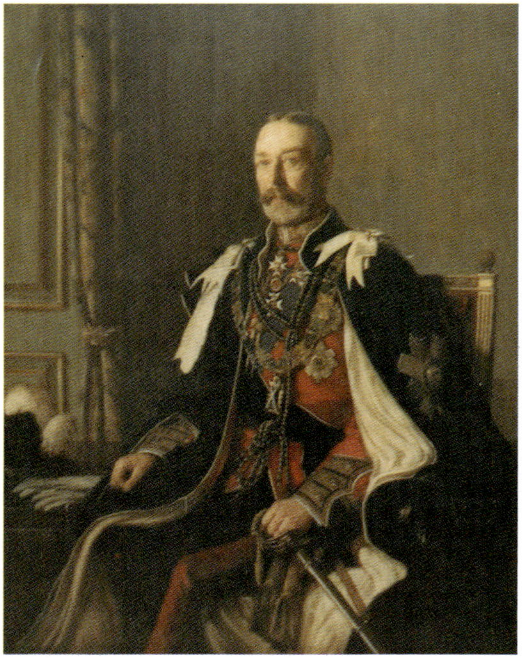

20. "King George V" was painted in 1932. The first sketch is in Beverley Art Gallery and the actual painting hangs in the throne room of Holyrood House, Edinburgh. Reproduced by gracious permission of Her Majesty The Queen.

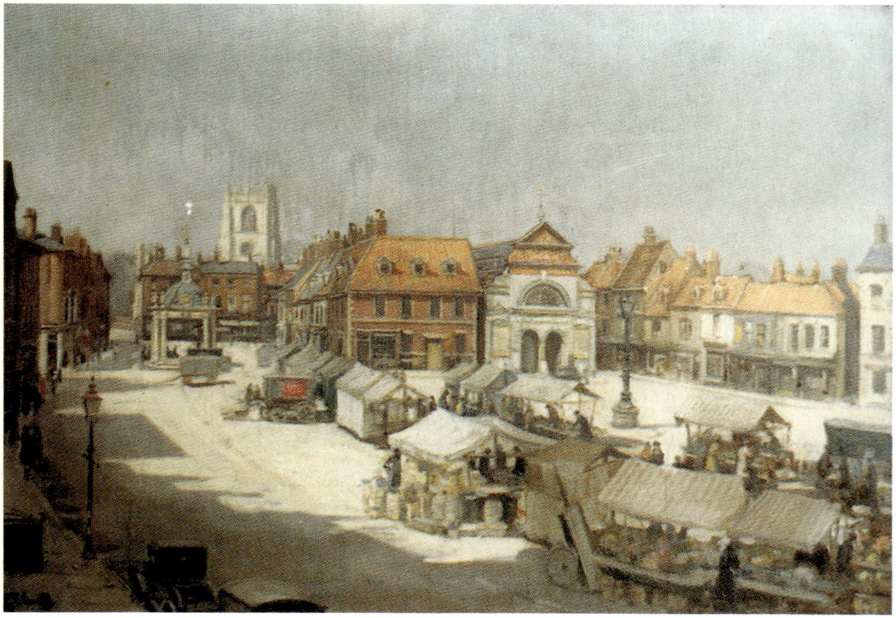

25. "Saturday Market" Beverley in 1935. Photograph courtesy of Alison Balding.

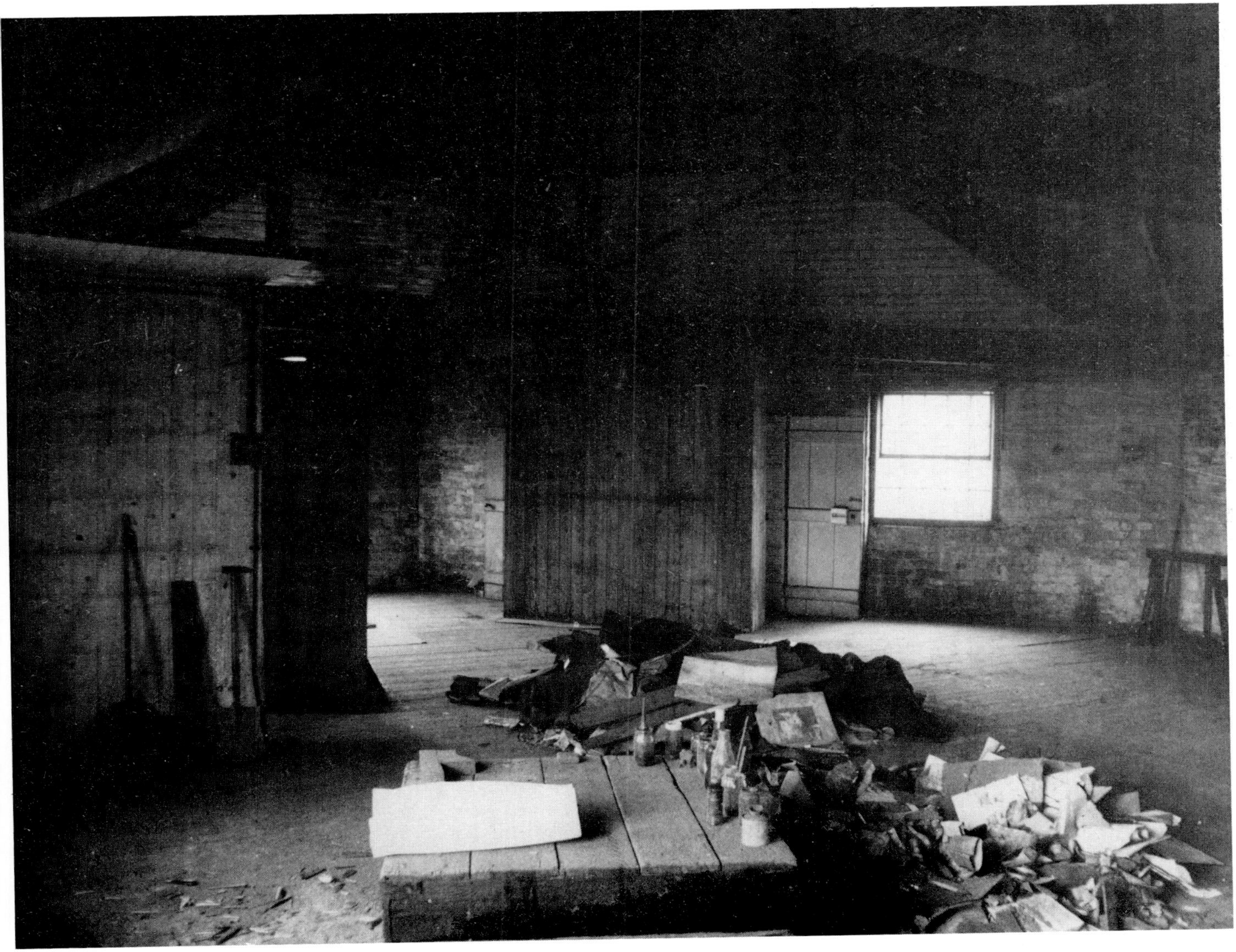

26. Photograph of the Trinity Lane studio in 1976 with piles of discarded canvasses.

THE ELWELL TRAIL

The trail can be covered in under two hours, but there are so many points of interest that it could equally take all day. However several places of refreshment are included!

Start at the Library in Champney Road. Upstairs is the:-

(1) Art Gallery

(Closed 12.30 - 2; Thursdays and Saturdays - mornings only), the home of the largest single collection of the paintings of Fred and Mary Elwell. Unless there is an exhibition in the Gallery, there are usually several Elwells on show and many more in the store-room. Many paintings were bequeathed in Fred's will and some have been donated or bought by the Borough Council. There is also a screen on loan from the Art Society on which several oil sketches for Fred's paintings can be discerned. Elwell's palette was found in his old Trinity Lane studio in 1976 and donated by Richard Wilson.

On leaving the Library, turn right and right again and walk along Lord Roberts Road. Turn right into Highgate towards the:-

(2) Minster

(usually open 9 a.m. to 5 p.m.). Fred painted many Minster interiors such as *Evensong* and *Lord Kitchener's Memorial Service* as well as exteriors from Hall Garth, Keldgate Manor Garden and at various times of the day. Look for the choir screen in the Minster carried out by James Elwell's firm. James was Fred's father and twice mayor of Beverley.

As you leave the Minster, turn right and then left into Eastgate. Now you can either walk through the new housing development near the old Friary, or continue along Eastgate and turn right at the Oddfellows Arms, into Trinity Lane. Next to the *Telegraph* public house is an old warehouse which was the:-

(3) Trinity Lane Studio

a setting for many pictures and a retreat for Fred. In 1932, the robes of the Order of the Thistle were kept here secretly guarded by nephew Kenneth Elwell so that Fred could complete the portrait of King George V.

Cross Station Square and turn left into Railway Street. Walk along to Wednesday Market, turn right into Butcher Row, Toll Gavel and into Saturday Market. In the corner of the Market Place is the:-

(4) Kings Head Hotel

whose Bandroom was the setting for the Beverley Band pictures including *Silver and Gold*, *Practice Night* and *Beverley Brass Band.*

Across the Market Place stands the Corn Exchange building housing the:-

(5) Playhouse

Mr. Ernest Symmons who owned the cinema for many years also made films including *Beverley Through the Ages* recording a pageant in 1937 in which Fred played the part of the Earl of Hastings.

To the right of the Playhouse is Ladygate. Continue along here until you reach Hengate and St. Mary's Church. Then left to visit the church of:-

(6) St. Mary's

(open daily, times vary). On the wall just before St. Michael's Chapel, is a painting of the chapel by Mary Elwell. When the roof was restored in 1939, a panel with a portrait of King George VI by Kenneth Elwell was placed in the Chancel ceiling.

Retrace your steps along Hengate down to the traffic lights passing on the way:-

(7) Arden's Vaults

a painting of which was exhibited at the Royal Academy in 1945. Extra pillars have been added to the public house scene. Further along is:-

(8) The White Horse

or ***Nellies*** which was the setting for the *Landlord*, owned by the Ferens Art Gallery in Hull.

Across the road the Dancewear & Theatrical Centre owned by a branch of the Elwell family, is close to:-

(9) 7 Hengate

formerly the home of Madge and Richard Whiteing, friends of the Elwells. The house was the setting of domestic interiors by both Fred and Mary.

Turn left at the traffic lights and walk along Manor Road, turning left at the roundabout into Wylies Road, formerly known to some as *Ticklebelly Alley*! Walk to the corner and look up at:-

(10) the door panels and carvings done by James Elwell's firm, based on Punch cartoons. *The Political Cheapjack* shows Disraeli prepared to give up liberal principles. Foreman W.J. Thorley has his name above the wood-carver's shop in the background. The other has Gladstone restraining 4 leashed dogs — the Labour, Nationalist, Radical and Parnellite parties and is entitled *Will They Work?*

There are more examples of the Elwell firm's work on *Pinewood* and *The Oak House* across the road in North Bar Without.

Look across to the:-

(11) Bar House

which incorporates the Guardroom above the Bar. Fred lived here for over 40 years. There is a plaque beside the front door. Look along North Bar Within which Fred regarded as the *loveliest street in England* and identify the doorway used in *The Last Cab* (Beverley Art Gallery). *The Birthday Party*, *The Window Seat* and many interiors were set in the Bar House. Fred was keen on the garden and this was also a favourite subject.

Walk along North Bar Within passing:-

(12) St. Mary's Court

formerly *Armstrong's Garage* exhibited at the Royal Academy in 1921 and was *A Munitions Factory* in 1944.

Proceed to the:-

(13) Beverley Arms Hotel

The *Elwells* bar celebrates their famous regular customer and has several reproductions of paintings and some photographs of Fred. The Hotel was the setting for many pictures including *Elevenses*, *An Inn Kitchen*, *Maid Plucking a Goose*, *The Beverley Arms Kitchen*, *Girl Polishing Pans*, and *The Pot Boy*. The kitchen is now the Shires Lounge. Look behind the reception desk for an original Elwell.

Turn right out of the hotel and head back to Saturday Market, passing Wood Lane where Fred had his first exhibition in the Old Quaker Chapel in 1899.

(14.) Fletchers

shop on the right, formerly Greens had an upstairs room used by the Beverley Art Club formed in 1955 at Fred's instigation.

Retrace your steps along Toll Gavel, turn right into Cross Street and right again into Register Square, with the:

(15) Guildhall

facing you. The Guildhall houses the Tourist Information office (open Monday to Saturday 9.30 - 6, Sunday 9.30 - 1.30). Some of Fred's works are hung here. *James Mills* and *The Courtroom* with Mary in a green dress, are over the staircase and Messrs. Champney, Wray and Spencer are in the Magistrates' Room. A pastel of George Monkman, aged over 90, as the *Macebearer* hangs in the Mayor's parlour.

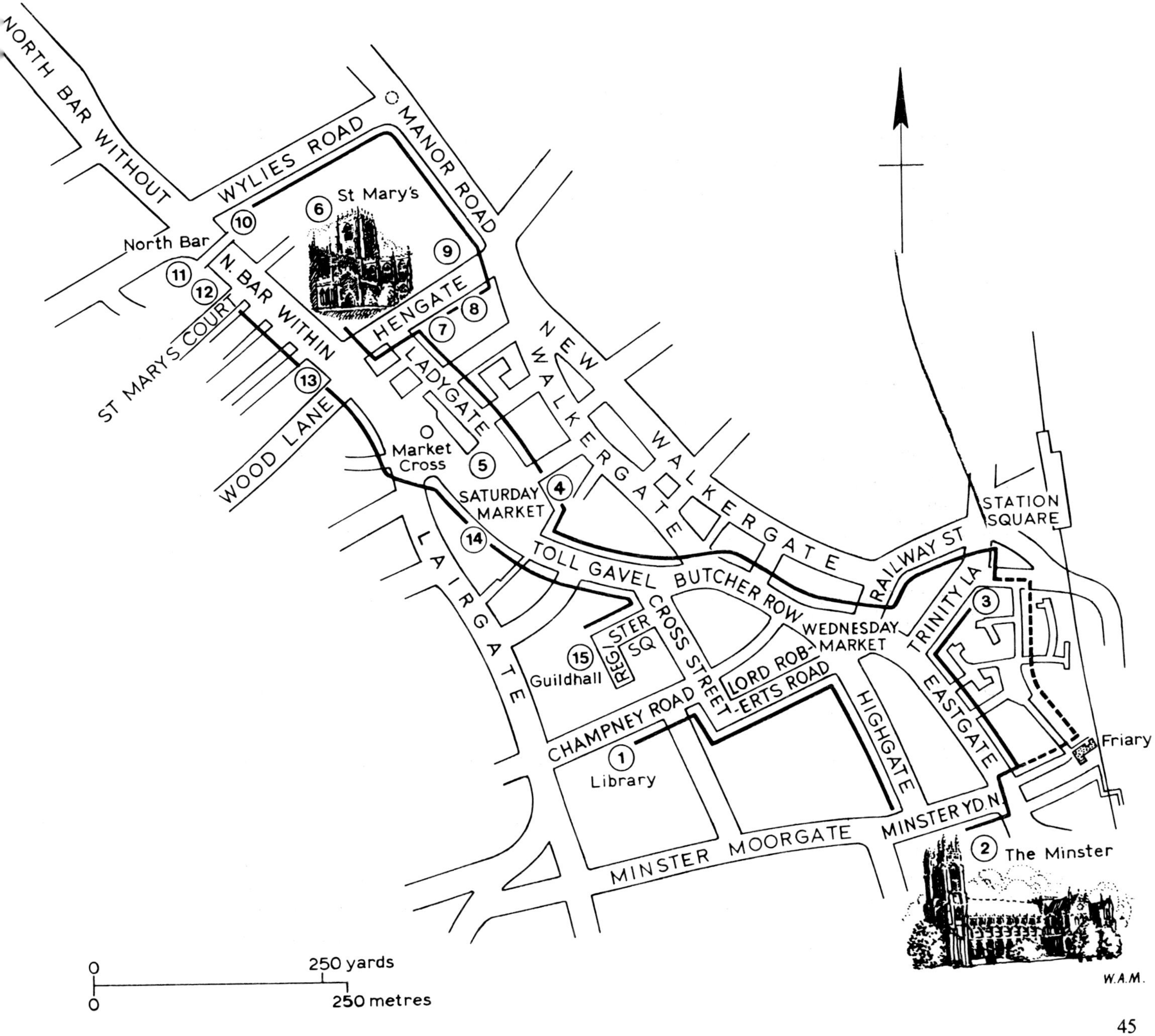
NORTH BAR WITHOUT
WYLIES ROAD
MANOR ROAD
St Mary's
North Bar
N. BAR WITHIN
ST MARYS COURT
HENGATE
LADYGATE
NEW WALKERGATE
WALKERGATE
WOOD LANE
Market Cross
SATURDAY MARKET
TOLL GAVEL
BUTCHER ROW
LAIRGATE
CROSS STREET
REG. SQ
STER
Guildhall
CHAMPNEY ROAD
LORD ROBERTS ROAD
HIGHGATE
WEDNESDAY MARKET
RAILWAY ST
STATION SQUARE
TRINITY LA
EASTGATE
Friary
Library
MINSTER MOORGATE
MINSTER YD.N.
The Minster
1
2
3
4
5
6
7
8
9
10
11
12
13
14
15
0
250 yards
0
250 metres
W.A.M.